J. S. Parker

Communication In Marriage

End the Fighting Once And For All

The Ultimate Guide For Couples Who Desire A Transformed and Blissful Marriage

J. S. PARKER

J. S. Parker

Copyright © 2016 J. S. PARKER

All rights reserved.

DEDICATION

This Book Is Dedicated To All The Wonderful Couples Out There Who Desire To Have A Transformed Marriage Filled With Pride, Happiness, Passion, Love, And Intimacy.

J. S. Parker

J. S. Parker

CONTENTS

Introduction	1
Chapter 1: Why Is A Passion-Filled Marriage Important?	3
Chapter 2: Secret Key #1 – Communication and Understanding	9
Chapter 3: Secret Key #2 – Being Open-Minded	16
Chapter 4: Secret Key #3 – Making Time For Yourselves	25
Chapter 5: Secret Key #4 – Being Intimate with One Another	40
Chapter 6: Secret Key #5 – Finding A Common Interest	62
Chapter 7: Special Useful Tips	72
BONUS BOOK: Relationship Breakthrough Table of Contents	77
End of Book	178

J. S. Parker

J. S. Parker

INTRODUCTION

Are you in a marriage that is leaving you lost and confused? Do you feel like the intimacy is fading? Are you just looking for a way to strengthen your bond with your spouse? If you have then you have purchased the right book. In this book, you will find out more about how these 5 keys can help you attain an intimate and passion-filled relationship that is founded on communication, love, and respect.. Find out what these keys are and what are the accompanying secrets that they will unlock in your partner and your marriage. You will be inspired to make these changes once you realize how simple yet how commonly overlooked these aspects are in any relationship. Do not make the mistake that most couples make and start picking up these keys and using them like they were always meant to be used.

This book is catered to those who strive to become more intimate and passionate with their partner. If you knew the secrets to unlocking the potential in your marriage, the level of intimacy will never be the same again. Be one of those special individuals that serve as a catalyst towards a better marriage for you and your spouse even if he or she does not even recognize there is a problem. If you resonate at all with the above, please read on to find out more about how to make that strong marriage happen.

Everyone needs this book. Whether you are married, currently in a relationship, wanting to get in one, or more.. It is the difference between a mediocre relationship and a phenomenal one.

CHAPTER 1

WHY AN INTIMATE AND PASSION-FILLED MARRIAGE IS IMPORTANT?

Any marriage must have passion and intimacy to succeed. You can't have a marriage where you two are complacent with each other. That is when the problems set in with infidelity, boredom, and sometimes, even divorce. Use this book as a tool to keep these problems at bay.

Don't get me wrong every marriage has its problems, but when you are passionate about each other, those problems seem minuscule, and they are a lot easier to get over than if you are bored with each other.

What a Passion-filled Marriage is Like

Imagine a marriage where you are gone all day, and all you can think about is rushing home to be with your spouse, just like in the honeymoon phase of your marriage. Now, imagine that you are still wanting to do that after ten years of marriage. The feeling of butterflies in your stomach at the thought of seeing your lover's face after a long day of work is unmatched by any other feeling in the world.

An intimate relationship is filled with love and compassion for the other person, but it is also interesting. It is never knowing what surprises lie in store, but trusting your partner, knowing they will be good.

Have you read any adult novels? The steamy, hot, romantic ones? Imagine having a marriage like that, twenty years into the future of your marriage. It may be unthinkable now, but after you read this book, and apply these five keys to your life, and your marriage, this will be your life.

Why You Should Strive for This

Marriage isn't easy. It comes with a myriad of

challenges and obstacles that you have to overcome. That is a part and parcel of marriage. What's not so good is if your marriage comes to a point that you end up being bored with your partner, this is a red flag that you need to quickly address. You definitely do not want to wait until the point that boredom leads to a black and gray picture. You want to add the colors back before it starts fading and to make it the most beautiful picture ever seen. Able to visualize and recall what a scene of that nature looks like? Fascinating isn't it?

Well what can happen if you do not address the problems and obstacles that arise in your marriage early on? Well on the top of my head, boredom can easily lead to infidelity. Ever felt that you were yearning for someone else to fulfill the needs that you have? Well that's not a good sign right there. That feeling stem from your spouse now shouldn't it?

Infidelity is not the only problem that stems from

boredom. Constant bickering is another one that can be detrimental to marriages. Once you get bored with someone, you begin to want something more to interest you, and you may start nitpicking at little things that don't even really bother you. Like the fact that your spouse left a spoon unwashed in the sink. You take that little issue and turn it into a full out fight because you are so tired of the silence. The funny thing is, you probably don't even realize that you are doing it either. You just subconsciously want to ease the constant humdrum feeling of the household.

Along with these, boredom can split your marriage apart. You just don't want to be with someone who is not passionate about you. So you decide to leave. You leave the person you love, and break your own heart, because you can't stay another minute in a lackluster relationship. Divorce is expensive, so maybe you just separate for a while, but it still takes its toll on your family. Especially if you have kids.

An intimacy filled relationship is key for a long successful marriage. If you are intimate and passionate about each other, then you will find a whole new world out there waiting for you to reach out for it. This world is full of fun adventures and happiness.

What to Expect From This Book

In this book you will find the next five chapters are the Keys to a passionate marriage. Each chapter is a different key. You have to read on to find out what those keys are. That is why it is called a secret. Each of the keys will have information to help you understand more how to go about using that key to unlock another section of your marriage. There will be different scenarios for some keys that may involve separate information for couples with kids, couples trying for kids, and couples without kids.

There will also be a chapter towards the end on what to expect once the honeymoon is over for newlyweds. This chapter can be skipped if you already have passed that phase in your marriage.

There will also be a chapter on how to recognize if your relationship is unhealthy, or just on the rocks, and information on how to leave a relationship if it is unhealthy/ abusive.

Why You Need These Keys

These keys unlock secret parts of a marriage that only a handful of couples have managed to reach. Without them you can have a normal marriage, and even one filled with love, but to truly be at a level beyond your peers and the average couple, you need to master these keys and locks to truly be in the stratosphere of your relationship. Do note that every relationship is different, and that everyone goes through unique circumstances that cannot be accounted for and addressed for every situation. You will have to adapt the scenarios in this book to fit your life. Ultimately you will have to discover what works and how best to implement it. I will do my best to make it very practical and applicable to most scenarios, giving you examples and case studies to illustrate the points that I am driving home. Okay enough of the jibber jabber. Now here comes the fun part! Read on to find out what each key is, and why you need it to make your marriage just that much more special.

CHAPTER 2

SECRET KEY #1

Communication and Understanding

This is perhaps the most important key in any successful happy and passionate relationship. Without this as a foundation, it is difficult to build on other facts that brings out the best in your relationship with your spouse. I decided to put it first, front and center so that you will remember it better.

Simply put, communication and understanding are

keys that most people don't even realize the importance of. This one isn't fully a secret, but the depth of it is. Sixty percent of couples do not realize that communication is about more than what you want to eat, and how you are feeling that day. Communication is telling you partner your favorite color, what your first bike looked like, and if you sucked your thumb as a kid. All the little details you would find odd that anyone would want to know, is everything that your partner should know, and vice-versa.

Understanding goes beyond being okay when someone makes a human mistake. Understanding is having the compassion to anticipate the needs of your spouse, while also realizing they are human and can be irrational. It is wanting to know why they sucked their thumb as a child. It is wanting to know what causes their nightmares. It is wanting to be there for them every step of the way in life. That is understanding.

Without these two elements in their fullest, you cannot truly know your partner. You will not be able to truly live in harmony, because you will not be able to understand why they do some of the things they do, and you will not be able to communicate why you are frustrated. This key unlocks compassion. True compassion for another person. The kind you wish the world would show you.

Communication is a big key in a marriage, because without it, you don't know what the other person is thinking. You aren't a mind reader, and you should not be expected to be. So you have to communicate. You have to speak up about what you are thinking. Whether it be if the other person hurt you, or if you want something. You can't get mad at someone for not doing something they had no idea they were supposed to be doing.

The other side of that discussion is you also have to be understanding when your partner is telling you something. It is really hard for communication to flow freely, when your spouse is afraid to tell you something, because they are afraid that you will get mad.

Understanding your partner also goes deeper than just being understanding. You also have to understand their wants and needs. Eventually you will learn to anticipate those, but for now, you have to focus on what they are trying to say, even if they aren't able to fully express it themselves. This goes for in and out of the bedroom. You have to love your spouse enough to learn everything about them, that way you can understand them better.

You are probably needing a lot more information on these subjects, so they will be broken down with more information, starting with communication.

Communication

Have you ever been mad at your spouse for not being romantic enough, or not taking out the trash or doing the dishes? Chances are you probably have. Think back to the last time you were angry at your spouse for something like that. Did you tell them that you wanted it done? No? Then why are you angry? It's not like they were ignoring you. Your spouse didn't know that he or she was supposed to do these things because you did not specify your desire for them to be done.

Lack of communication leads to unnecessary fighting, and that makes your household miserable, and a miserable household is not one filled with passion. You have to talk to your partner. There are many ways to begin telling them what is bothering you, if you are not sure how to begin.

You can start by writing everything down, and giving

it to them. This may seem like a juvenile thing to do, but if you are not great at expressing desire or emotions, it is a helpful tool that will allow you to get everything out without a problem. They also can't interrupt you, because you aren't physically speaking. Writing your feelings down can also help you decide if you are being irrational. It is actually a good idea to write them down, even if you plan on speaking your mind, because you can make yourself sound more rational to save saying something that you will regret.

If you can communicate rationally, then you can sit down, and have a heart-to-heart chat about things that are bothering you. Take turns saying your what's on your mind and take turns listening to your partner's. Sometimes, you feel a lot better getting it off your chest, rather than just bottling it up. Because when you bottle something up, it just builds and builds and builds, until you finally snap. This is the cause of a lot of problems, because you snap at your partner for no apparent reason, due to the fact that you are just now showing anger over something that happened two weeks ago.

However, if you fight over everything, and even written communication doesn't help, then you can try a technique that has helped save many marriages. You schedule an argument where you plan to get everything out on the table that has made you angry recently. Before you start the argument, buy a couple of helium-filled balloons. Roll a die to see who has the floor first. Highest number wins. Once you figure out who has the floor first, that person pokes a hole in their balloon and sucks the helium out. Be sure to pinch the hole closed while you are talking so the helium doesn't escape cause you are going to need to refill your lungs a couple of times.

Once you have filled your lungs with helium, it is time to start talking. Talk about everything that bothers you, big and small, until you start laughing. If you can't be angry about it while speaking in a chipmunk voice, then it wasn't worth getting angry in the first place. Once you both have said your piece, go over what you were angry enough about to say even though your voices were distorted hilariously. Try to find solutions to those problems. Once you can find a solution to your problems, you will be able to avoid having those same problems in the future.

Be Honest

Communication is not just calling out your spouse when they have done something wrong. It is also admitting when you mess up as well. If you make a mistake, tell your partner, and let them know how much you truly regret it.

Being honest is hard, but if you do or say something

that you know will hurt your partner to find out about, it is best to tell them yourself. If they hear it from someone else, it is liable to ruin your relationship. However, if they hear it from you directly, they may hurt for a while, but they will respect you for telling the, the truth.

However, honesty is not just about when you do something wrong, it is also about telling your partner the truth whether they want to hear it or not. Say you are a guy, and your wife is putting on her makeup. She finishes, and thinks she looks great, but it makes her look a little clownish. Kindly tell her that it is a bit much. Offer some suggestions to make it look better without her having to redo everything. As angry as she may be, it is better for you to tell her, than for her to hear it from some snickering strangers. If she decides to still go out like that, then it is her choice and you must support her, but you should always warn her first.

Say you are a woman, and your husband wears nothing but Hawaiian shirts and cargo shorts, and you wish he would wear something different once in a while. Be honest with him. Tell him you love him for who he is, but sometimes a change is refreshing. Offer some suggestions that he might like, and if he still refuses, accept it and move on. You cannot change them, but they don't know you don't like something unless you tell them.

Be honest about your plans. Don't tell your spouse that you are going somewhere, and be somewhere else entirely. Even if you think they will get mad about where you plan to go, it is always best to be honest, because if something were to happen to you, and you weren't where you say you were, they would have no idea where to start looking. You have to be open and forthcoming with information always, otherwise, you can break your partner's trust, or worse, you could get hurt and they wouldn't know what happened.

As difficult as it can be to be honest sometimes, it is necessary. You have to be truthful. If you are honest with your partner, it will strengthen their trust in you, and they will love you even more knowing that they can always count on you to do the right thing, no matter how hard it is.

Communication in its entirety can save a marriage, as you are getting things off your chest, and working to fix problems. Finding solutions together will bring you closer together as a couple, and ignite the passion in your marriage. You will find that things get a whole lot more steamy and intimate when you start opening up and being honest with each other.

Understanding Your Partner

Everyone has their quirks. We all have something that makes us different from everyone else. And while that is endearing, because it makes us unique, these quirks can also cause a problem in a marriage where couples don't understand them.

Early on in the marriage, during the honeymoon stage, everything is a wonderful bed of thorn-less roses. You get up, enjoy each other's company and are full of love for each other, but as you discover more and more about your partner, you find there are more and more things that you don't understand. This is normal. You are just learning about your partner, and you are not expected to know everything about them yet.

However, if something they do bothers you, ask them about it. Try to understand why it is that they do what they do. Understand who they are, and always understand that they are only human, they are not perfect.

Understanding Their Needs

Understanding your partner goes beyond understanding the things they do. It also branches out into understanding their needs, and being able to anticipate their wants. This does not come immediately and it takes some work. You have to communicate to get to this phase. Talk about what you like, and your hobbies, and what you want from life. There are basic needs however that you should know about. These needs differ between the sexes.

Men

Men are seen as tough, indestructible creatures because that is what society imposes on them. They are expected to be the breadwinners of the family, and to never show emotion. This is the farthest thing from the truth. Men need a safe place to show their emotions, and they too need a shoulder to cry on at times.

Men need to feel validated. They need to be told how important they are, and not be taken for granted. Society dictates that a man already know how important he is and that he is an egotistical brute. Society is wrong. Often times men are just as insecure as women. They need to be told how good they look, and be told that they are appreciated.

Men go through a lot. They work hard all day to help pay the bills (in most cases). They come home, and love on their spouses, and if they have them, children. They just want to sit in a chair and eat dinner and then go to sleep. However, doing this can lower a man's self-esteem, as he feels he is letting the household down. Men need an extra chore around the house to feel like they are helping their spouses, even if the spouse doesn't work. Ask him to take out the trash. He will groan about it, but deep down he will enjoy doing something that makes your life a little easier.

In turn, you should make his life a little easier. Don't complain about every little thing. This is where understanding comes in. Rather than complain, voice your concerns kindly, and help try to find solutions to the problems. This makes the household a less stressful environment, and makes it more enjoyable.

Men are seen as creatures that always want sex. This is not always true. However, if he wants sex often and you don't, don't gripe at him on a day where you want sex and he doesn't. If you are allowed to not be in the mood, so is he. It does not mean he is cheating on you. Chances are, if he has a high libido, he just rubbed one out right before you asked, and is embarrassed to tell you. Or maybe he just had a bad day, and just wants to cuddle and talk about it. Be there for him like he is there for you.

There are a lot more needs that men have, but those are more controversial. Just be there for him. Your husband needs to feel loved and secure in your marriage. This is one thing that doesn't change across the board.

Women

Women are very strong beings. While that is very much true, there are times when women also want to have the chance to be vulnerable and to depend on their man. With that said, it is statistically proven that women don't want their men to be to clingy. So bottom-line, guys please know your boundaries well. For the following points that I am going to make, I will make a quick note now to acknowledge that each women is special, different, and unique in her own right. To break things down simpler for the masses, these are basic and generalized needs that women have.

Women need as much, if not more validation then men. They constantly are under a barrage of pressure to by society to be an act in a certain way. Society puts so much pressure on women to look perfect, and be perfect, that if they don't live up to those standards, it can be tough on them. As her spouse, it is your job to make her feel like she is perfect. Even if her hair is a mess, and she hasn't shaved her legs in a couple of days.

Women are insecure at times as well. Think back to the Taylor Swift song "Mine". Yes I've heard and watched the music video. If you haven't, go watch it and you'll understand what I mean. Oops let's not get sidetracked. Yes please assure your girl that you are going to stick by her side forever, even when things get rough.

Women need to be held too! Cuddling creates endorphins in the brain that give humans a burst of happiness. These endorphins are drained from a woman's system faster than they are for a man. So she needs to be cuddled more than you realize. If she is having a bad day, suggest she take a break from whatever she is doing and come cuddle with you for fifteen minutes. You would be surprised how much difference such a little break will make.

I don't really want to bring out biology but let's address it head on because, well, why shouldn't we? Now as we all know women go through "that time of the month"; pregnancy, and menopause. *Flashback to a particular Modern Family episode*. These scenarios cause hormonal imbalances in women resulting in discomfort, pain, and mood swings. With that in mind, it is the man's job to be understanding of this. Offer to clean the house for her, or go pick up her favorite meal. This is a way you can show that you love her, and give her what she needs. Offer to pick up any sanitary products she needs. Simple gestures like that make a world of difference to a female. REMEMBER THIS. Also be understanding if she wakes you up at three in the morning to go get her some chicken wings. She can't help it.

Women need to feel protected. They need to feel like nothing in the world is ever going to hurt them ever again. Chances are, she has had a fair share of heartbreak before she met you. Don't break her heart too. Be her superhero, and vow to protect her from evil. Even just saying it while pulling her into a hug will make a huge impact on her. When she feels safe in the relationship, she will open up more and talk about what bothers her, rather than keep it bottled up until she snaps. Chris Daughtry's Song "Superman" would pretty much sum up this whole paragraph. Go take a listen, I'm sure you'll like it.

Women need to feel important in your life. Even if nothing major happened, she needs to feel like she was a part of it. Tell her about your day, give her details of what happened, even if they were boring. Talk about how you missed her while you were at work, and describe an interesting person you saw at work that day.

Women need to be loved. They need romance. This doesn't mean drop a thousand dollars a week on her. It can be small things like planning a picnic, bringing her some flowers that you picked from a field. Cooking dinner for her after she had a long day, or bring her breakfast in bed. She just needs some effort put into it. Even if it doesn't cost a dime. Adam Levine knows this best in "She Will Be Loved".

Now now I get that I'm making a lot of popular culture music references. But hey sometimes music captures very important elements that resonates with us longer in our minds because we listen to them over and over again. We subconsciously absorb the content and unconsciously act on them too. So do find songs that drive home the points that I'm making because I'm sure you'd enjoy listening to them as much as you like reading about them. They are a perfect complement to one another. Am I right or am i right?

Okay so Why again this Key is Important?

You need to understand and truly know your spouse, that way you can anticipate any problems that may arise. You will be in blissful peace if you can use this key to unlock the ability to solve problems before they start. And you will also unlock a compassion rivaled only by that of a small child watching someone cry.

CHAPTER 3

SECRET KEY #2

Be Open Minded

This is the second key you need to own. Most people don't know that marriage is based on being willing to listen to what your partner has to say with an open heart. Over eighty five percent of people say that they would not budge their values to please a spouse. However, sometimes you have to budge a little bit, to unlock the raw emotion in your spouse that you really need to access to be close to them. You should want to know every part of them without judging them, for only then can you reach the depths of their soul that no one else has been to.

Marriage is a whole lot of give and take. There is not much that you can have exactly how you want it. In marriage, you often find out things about the other person that you didn't know when you were dating, and you have to be prepared for this shock. You can't be mad at a person for not showing you everything in the this lovey phase of your relationship with them. They could jolly-well be concealing that side of themselves so as to present to you the best impression that they can give to you. Time will unlock the vulnerable and raw side of your spouse. So give it time and be open about it.

You have to be willing to accept them even after they have told you about themselves, and you have found out things that may not be to pleasant. These things could be as small as them having having a quirky way of eating their food, to major mind-blowing facts like discovering how many partners they have been with prior to marrying you. Remember when you said "I do"? You promised to take your spouse for the good and the bad. So you have to be prepared for anything.

Here are some scenarios in the form of mini fiction stories that should help you understand more what it means to be open minded. These stories are different for the types of families out there whether they have kids or not. There is one scenario for every type of classification of family.

Couples with Kids

Scenario

Stacy had just married her boyfriend of six years two months ago, and the honeymoon phase was just starting to fade. She was shocked that there even was a honeymoon phase to begin with, seeing as she had lived with her husband Josh for five years before they were married, and they had two kids together. She felt that they had already been through everything they could have gone through together. She took a peak into her room to look at her sleeping husband and sighed with happiness. She repeated the action while peeking into her kids rooms. Stacy was happy, and she felt that nothing could spoil her life.

Stacy was far from right with that thought. Later that day, an officer arrived at her door. Stacy was confused, as she didn't have any idea why he would be there. Then she saw another officer standing there holding a baby in a car-seat.

"Josh! Get out here please!" she called down the hallway to her husband's office where he was busy working.

Her kids came out of the room to investigate, but Stacy sent them back. Josh came down the hall and stopped dead in his tracks when he saw the officers and the baby.

"What is going on here?" He asked

The officer that knocked on the door stepped forward, and offered his hand to shake with the couple. They took it and shook it briefly.

"I'm Officer Jennings, and this here is Officer Saul" Officer Jennings gestured to the other officer who was holding the infant, before continuing the conversation. "I'm sure you have a lot of questions, but let me get through explaining the situation to you before you ask, do we have a deal?"

"Yes" Josh and Stacy replied in unison

"Three days ago, a woman by the name of Allisson Marx passed away in childbirth. Doctors told her early on she probably would not survive giving birth, but she decided to go ahead with the pregnancy anyways. She noted the birth father, and ask that he be notified if she did pass. The birth father is noted here as Josh Layman. The same Josh Laymen that is noted to live at this address. She has also left a number for you to call. As you are the father you have to either sign over custody, or claim custody. You have to wait three days to sign over custody however, as this is a long weekend, and all the offices are closed. We are required to give you custody until you are able to make a decision. Now, any questions?"

After Stacy and Josh asked their questions, the officers left, leaving the baby and a few boxes of diapers and formula, along with informing them of the child's name.

" How did this happen?! And don't give me some smart ass answer. I know how this happened, I just want to know when and why!" Stacy asked adamantly.

"Mommy? Can we come out now?" Her oldest son asked.

"Not right now sweetie. Mommy and Daddy are having a grown up discussion"

"Okay Mommy."

Josh turned to Stacy. I know you are angry. And you have every right to be. But it isn't what you think. I didn't cheat on you. I got with Allisson when we separated over a year ago. I dated her almost the entire five months we were separated. I had no idea she was pregnant though. I know you are probably really angry, but this is my child. I don't want to sign over my rights to her."

Discussion

Stacy has one of two options here. She could force Josh to either give up the baby or lose her and his other kids, or she could be open-minded, and accept this child as her own. Let's talk about the consequences of each action, starting with the first.

If she were to give Josh an ultimatum, he would either sign over the rights to the child he doesn't know and lose the two he does, along with his new wife. He would probably chose to sign over the baby.

If he signed over that child, he would spend the rest of their marriage blaming her, and resenting his other kids, because he never got the chance to know his daughter. This would cause a major rift in their relationship, and could potentially destroy it, and that would leave their marriage the same as it would have been if he refused to sign over the rights.

However, if Stacy is open-minded, she will realize that while her husband had been with another woman, they were not together, and had agreed to see other people at that time, so he really did nothing wrong. She could also have a wonderful addition to her new family, and get to watch another beautiful baby grow up. She could have a daughter along with her two sons, and though that baby girl didn't come from her, she could grow to love that child as much as her biological children.

Being open-minded can save their marriage, and even add to it. Though the child was unexpected, being able to take her in and love her unconditionally will make them stronger as a family, and her compassion will ignite a fire in Josh's heart, which will in turn reignite the flame in hers.

Couples Trying to Have Children

Scenario

Layne and Michal Sherwood had been married for three years before they decided to try to have children. Michal was adamant that he and Layne have only biological children. He refused to adopt, because he wanted his children to be his and his alone. He didn't want someone else's kids. Michal was excited when Layne said that she was ready to try to have kids. They tried for two years, suffering two miscarriages, before they finally decided to go to a specialist.

"Mr. and Mrs. Sherwood? I am Dr. Branston" an elderly man came in and shook their hands before continuing "I am afraid I have some bad news. We ran several tests, and have confirmed that not only are you ninety percent infertile Mr. Sherwood, but Mrs. Sherwood, you are unable to carry a child full term due to a poorly angled uterus. This is the first case I have had in fifteen years that we couldn't at least use a surrogate in. I am sorry to say that naturally having kids is just not in the cards for you two." and with that the doctor left, and a nurse showed them out of the office.

When they got home, Michal was furious. He never wanted to have to adopt but it seemed that adopting was his only option. His wife wanted a family as well, so he couldn't just think about what he wanted.

Discussion

Now Michal could refuse to adopt, and they could live out their lives without a child, but that is not the life they want to live. They both want children. If Michal refuses to change his mind, he could potentially lose his wife of five years, because he was too stubborn to be open-minded.

However if he chooses to adopt, he can bring a joy and a wonderful passion into his family, and it could bring him and his wife closer, because they will not only have a child, they can bring happiness to a child's life that may not have had that happiness otherwise.

Being open-minded in this scenario can give this couple the family they want, and can bring them closer together, as they tackle an obstacle together.

Couple Without Children

This scenario is completely different, as there are no children involved whatsoever.

Scenario

Scott and Casey have been married for two years. When they started dating, Scott voiced his distaste for tattoos and piercings, and Casey told him that she loved them. He told her that they were gross, and for a while she shoved down her obsession with them to try to make them happy.

One day, Casey decided that she needs to do what makes her happy, so she goes and gets a tattoo. She had tried to understand why her husband didn't like them, but he could give no other explanation other than they were not natural. She tried being open-minded and seeing things his way, but soon she realized that he had no reason not to like them other than just being judgmental, so she started pressing for a tattoo, and piercings. Her husband forbade her from getting them.

Casey was so angry at being told she was not allowed to do something with her own body that she went and got a tattoo. She decided she was tired of letting her husband control her.

When she got home, her husband was really angry. He yelled at her for hours before finally calming down.

Discussion

Scott has two options here. He can either leave her

because she disobeyed a direct order, or he can be open-minded and listen to why she wanted the tattoo in the first place.

If he leaves her over a tattoo, he is throwing away two years of a great marriage because he was too stubborn to realize that his wife was her own person, and in control of her own body. This would be the biggest mistake he ever made, because looks change, but the heart never does, and while his wife had new ink, she was still the same loving person he married.

However, if he actually opens his mind, and decides to listen to why she wanted the tattoos and piercings, and accepts her for who she is, she will love him even more, for making an effort to be loving and accepting of things he didn't like. And maybe, he will eventually come to love her tattoos and piercings, as he loves her. He may even want a few of his own. You never know.

Recap

Those are the three scenarios that could happen, and how to handle them. These are just examples of what could happen. As stated above, every situation is different. If you are open minded, then you can learn more about your partner, and maybe, just maybe, you will find that you actually love these things.

Being open-minded is very important in a marriage, because the willingness to step out of your comfort zone makes it clear that you love that person more than yourself, which only makes them love you more. Passion stems from seeing things that make you fall in love all over again.

Try New Things

Being open minded is not just about being accepting of things that you don't agree with, it is learning to love things that your partner loves. There are a lot of things out there that you may not love, and that is okay, but if your partner loves it, then you should try to show an interest in it.

You and your spouse are two different people, and while you probably have a few common interests, you probably also have some things that you like that aren't shared by your spouse. That is okay. Your spouse probably has things that you don't particularly care for either. However, unless it is an unhealthy habit, you should never tell them they need to quit their hobby. You should always support your spouse to the fullest when they enjoy something.

It is also good to try to learn more about what they enjoy. Ask them to teach you more about what they enjoy, and watch their face light up like a kid on their birthday opening presents. Just knowing that you are trying to enjoy what they enjoy is enough to make them want to take you in their arms and show you how much they love you right then and there.

Showing your partner that you care about what they are doing, and what they enjoy, even if you don't really enjoy those things yourself will make them love you even more, because you are making an effort to join them in their happiest times. Ask them to talk about their passion, and really watch them as they talk about it. Listen to the excitement as they get into explaining something about it, and how much brighter their eyes get as they babble on and on about it. Ask questions, and don't make them ever feel like you are bored. But I guarantee you, that even if their passion is watching grass grow, you will not be bored watching them talk about it. The way they let go, and the raw excitement and happiness on their face will make you fall even more in love with your spouse. You get to see a side of them that few others get to see, and it will make you want to keep them talking for hours.

Trying new things can help your marriage, because

your spouse does not have to feel like they have to hide a part of themselves to be with you, and it will be a much happier environment. That happiness will turn into passion, and that passion will lead to more intimacy.

Why You Need This Key

This key is one of the most important keys in this book, because when someone feels that they can come to you without fear of judgment no matter what it is they need (or want) to say, it will create a bond filled with trust, and this will bring you closer together, as you learn more about each other, and allow each other deep within your minds, hearts and souls.

CHAPTER 4

SECRET KEY #3

Make Time for Yourselves

This key is needed to unlock parts of yourself, more than parts of your partner. It unlocks all the honeymoon feelings that you have stored away due to life trying to destroy them. Very few couples realize that time apart and time together apart from everything is needed to really fall in love with your spouse over and over again.

Life gets busy, and sometimes you don't realize that you haven't had any time to yourselves for a while. This section will include how to go about arranging alone time, both with each other, away from the rest of the world, and separate from each other.

Firstly, you need some time together away from the rest of the world. Life gets busy, especially if you are both working, and have conflicting schedules. However, you have to make time for each other, so that you can rekindle that spark every now and then.

Imagine this scenario. The characters will have names but you can substitute your own. Just relax and put yourself in this scene.

Scenario

Jillian smiled across the table at her husband. Tonight was the first night in over three years that they had been out on a date together. Between work, carpool, taking care of the kids, and just a plain busy life, they had not been able to enjoy each other's company for quite some time. That was until Alex, her wonderful husband, had set up this surprise.

Alex knew that his wife needed a break, so he figured what better time to do it, than over the long weekend? He kept the entire thing a secret, making sure that their two boys never said a word about spending a few days with their Uncle Ted. He set up reservations at a hotel so that his wife would not be tempted to use the quiet time to clean house. He got a table at a different nice restaurant for dinner all three nights. He had everything planned out, and it was being executed perfectly.

"How is dinner, my love?" Alex asked Jillian.

"It is wonderful, Dear." Jillian sighed with contentment.

Alex stared with wonder at his beautiful bride, and found himself falling in love with her all over again. She had forgone her usual bun for an elaborate up-do, and she had traded her usual old t-shirt and yoga pants for the red satin dress that had sat unworn in the closet for years. It still fit her as well as it did the last time she wore hit. His mind instantly went back to that night, and the passion that filled it. Almost four years ago, the night they conceived their youngest son. His trousers started to tighten at the thought of reliving that passion this weekend.

Jillian looked up and noticed her husband's eyes blazing with desire as he looked at her. She blushed. It had been awhile since he looked at her that way. Or maybe he had, and she just never noticed. But she had a feeling it had something to do with the fact that she wasn't in her usual housewife attire.

Jillian took some time to admire her husband as well. Instead of the sawdust covered t-shirt, dirty old work jeans, and scuffed boots, her husband had donned a three-piece suit she hadn't seen in a while. She admired the way it contoured against his body, showing off the muscles he had gained since starting his new job at a construction site. The pants cupped his rear quite nicely as well. She can't remember the last time he looked this fit. Not even the night that they conceived their youngest son, the most passion that they had ever seen in their marriage, the last time he wore that suit. She felt herself getting hot and flustered as she began to daydream herself back to that day.

"You look stunning tonight, baby." Alex said, breaking her reverie.

" As do you, darling" Jillian replied, smiling at Alex again.

They finished dinner, and went back to the hotel. They weren't quite ready to go in yet, so they walked through the hotel garden under the light of the full moon. Alex slid his arm around his wife's waist, and pulled her close to him. He couldn't stand not being able to see her face though, so he pulled her in front of him. Their bodies pressed together in the moonlight, he stared into her gorgeous blue-green eyes, and noted how rosy her cheeks were. Even though she wore only the slightest hint of makeup, her features were striking, and he wondered why he hadn't noticed how beautiful she had become since the birth of their last child. His wife had always been beautiful, but lately, Jillian had been working out to lose some of that stubborn baby weight. As sad as he was to see it go, he couldn't help but see how much happier she was with how she looked, and tonight it shined through.

Her happy face was the most beautiful thing he had ever seen, and he would do anything to keep that smile on her face. He leaned in for a kiss, and watched as her gorgeous eyes fluttered shut. Her long dark lashes cast half-moon shadows on her cheeks, and her perfect heart-shaped lips parted as she awaited the feel of his lips on hers. He kissed her softly, and felt the passion between them build. Their kiss ignited like a white hot fire, and he knew he needed to have her. Now. With deep regret, he pulled away from their kiss, and grabbed her hand as they ran back to the hotel. They were barely in the door, when she shoved him up against the door, and their lips met again, barely parting at all as they removed each other's clothes on the way to the bedroom.

Discussion

Jillian and Alex rekindled a passion that they haven't felt in three years. All it took was some time away from the world, for them to find the passion that the were missing in their lives. They fell in love again within a few hours of being alone, and they remembered why they got married in the first place.

Spending some time together away from everyone else is essential in a marriage. You have to have some time to really enjoy each other, or else you will begin to forget why you fell in love with each other. The daily routines you both have that take you in different directions put a lot of strain on your marriage, and if you go too long without having some time together, you begin to feel like strangers. You cannot function in a marriage if you feel that you do not know the person sleeping next to you.

There is also the matter of spending alone time by yourselves. You need some time to be you without anyone else. Some time to unwind and refresh. This may mean you take a hike for a few hours, or you go out to the club without your spouse or mutual friends. Maybe you curl up with a good book, and enjoy some peace and quiet. In this scenario, you will find how important some alone time really is.

Rachel was sitting on the greyhound looking out the window. She had been traveling for three days, trying to get back home. She left her husband in California, and was heading back home to Florida. As she sat on the bus she had a lot of time to think.

Juan was a loving husband, they were together all of the time, and everyone thought that their marriage was perfect, but the past several months they had been fighting constantly. They argued over every little thing. Their last argument, Juan got violent with her. He shoved her into the wall on the staircase landing, and then tripped her down the stairs. He had never been violent with her before, but she wasn't going to stand for it at all. In the middle of the night, she cleaned out her bank account, and bought a bus ticket home. She took nothing but a suitcase and a carry-on, and their six month old daughter.

She thought back to when things were great. That was before Juan lost his job, and she had to get a job. She found a job working from home for good pay, so that she was able to stay home due to being very pregnant. After Olivia was born, things started to go south. Juan refused to get up in the middle of the night with their daughter, and became very lazy. This caused fights. Rachel was stressed to the max with a newborn, a demanding job, and a husband who wouldn't step up to help. They fought more and more, until one day everything fell apart.

Now Rachel was sitting on a bus, her daughter in a carrier in the seat beside her, and she wonders if she did the right thing. There is never any excuse for violence in a relationship, but in their three years together that was the first instance of any violence, and he was horrified with himself after-wards.

Discussion

Juan and Rachel fought because they never had any time apart. Juan slept so much just to get some space from his wife, and thus he missed out on the time period needed to help his wife. The fights got worse, and Juan became more and more agitated, mostly at himself for not being able to find a new job, and one day he snapped.

While there is no excuse to get violent in a relationship, this could have been avoided if they had taken some time for themselves, rather than spend every waking moment together. The fights also could have been avoided if Juan had stepped up and helped with Olivia and the household, but that falls more under communication and understanding.

You need space in a relationship. Not only from the world, but from each other as well. You need to miss each other, and you need to have that time where you aren't working or taking care of kids, but you still have your space from each other as well. Just as you need regular date nights. Even if it is something inexpensive, you still need to take that time to rekindle the flame.

So no matter how busy your schedule is, make some

time to find yourself, and to rediscover your partner. No job, carpool, or dance recital is worth losing your marriage. And that isn't to say that kids aren't important, you just can't spend every single moment of your lives doting on them.

Go Out with Friends

You don't just need time alone and time apart, you also need friends outside of your children. (If you have children.) You need time away. Don't let anyone tell you that you are a bad parent because you need time away from your kids a couple nights a month, whether it be to unwind together, separate, or with friends. You are humans, and you deserve some space as well. You can't be expected to be a superhero, and be with your children all the time. They need to learn what it is like to be apart from you sometimes so that they don't develop separation anxiety. As long as you are not going out every weekend, there is no harm in some alone time. Go out. Have fun. Be free. Don't let anyone make you feel bad for being human.

Find some friends to go out to the bar with. Find some friends to go hiking with. Find friends that have common interests. Just find some people that you can go out with. They can have children or be child free, depending on the type of conversation you want to have. If you want a conversation that doesn't always steer towards kids, child free friends would be the way to go.

Bottom line of this chapter is: You are human, and need some time away from the world. You need to have fun, and unwind. Don't be afraid to act like a human, just because you are married doesn't mean the fun has to end.

Why You Need this Key

This key is instrumental in unlocking your old feelings for your partner. Back to the days where the passion ran wild, and your hearts were free from stress and sadness. Couples need this key if they want to feel like young lovers again.

CHAPTER 5

SECRET KEY #4

Intimacy

This is the chapter that may not be for some people, however, if you want your marriage to succeed and succeed extraordinarily, reading this chapter is imperative. Put your discomfort aside, and you may find you enjoy this chapter, along with some useful information to aid you in your marriage.

Make a Sex List

According to research, couples that have regular sex

are 75% more likely to have a successful marriage than couples who do not. Couples who are adventurous with sex are also 18% more likely to have a successful marriage than even those who have regular sex. This key is necessary to unlock the carnal parts of yourself and your partner that have never been touched before.

Sex is important in a marriage. Plain and simple. Not only is it used for procreation, it is a pleasurable bonding experience between you and your partner. However, it needs to go beyond the missionary stage eventually.

Think about the last time you had sex. Were you into it? Or did you just do it because you had the time, and you weren't sure when you would have the time again? Was it interesting? Or boring? If it felt forced and boring, it could be that you need to step out of your normal sex routine. This chapter will go over what goes into making sex fun and enjoyable for both parties, and what types of sex there are. Lastly, this chapter will go over how to make a sex list and what exactly you use a sex list for.

Enjoying Sex

It is important to enjoy sex with your partner. It should not feel forced, it should feel like a loving, passionate experience every time. Even if you are just having a quickie in the laundry room while your kids are downstairs watching television and waiting for their dinosaur nuggets to come out of the oven. It should feel like a dirty little secret that makes you blush every time you think of it, yet still gives you butterflies that make you want to do it again. The passion in your love making should rival that of the passion in a steamy adult novel.

This is achieved by several steps. You can't just throw

in a new position, and expect sex to feel phenomenal. It may be a little better, but there is more to sex than just the act itself. You have to mentally be in the zone as well as physically.

Foreplay

Foreplay is more than just a little kissing and oral sex. It is the time before sex that you use to clear your mind of everything but sex and breathing. You can't just kiss a few places and call it good. The best foreplay starts hours before the sex. Here are a few things you can do to make foreplay a part of your life.

FOREPLAY AT WORK-

Yes, that is correct. You can start foreplay even while both you and your partner are at work. On your breaks, and your lunch, text your partner all the things you want to do that night. Be descriptive and be forward. Don't beat around the bush making things confusing for your partner to figure out. The brashness of your texts will catch them off guard, and really turn them on. This is where you have to be careful though. Make sure you only text them on your breaks. You don't want to get in trouble from your boss because you are texting at work. Also, the added anticipation of getting to text them again makes the moment build.

Once you get home, the foreplay doesn't stop there. As you go about your daily chores, add in a few inappropriate touches here and there. Grab your partner's rear end, crotch or (if female), chest as you are walking by. These little naughty touches will leave you wanting more.

After dinner, and putting the kids to bed, if you have kids, take a shower together. Wash each other all over, taking explicit pleasure in the genital areas, and use the soap to stimulate your partner, and have them do the same. You can actually initiate sex in the shower as well if you wish, but sometimes it is nice to just keep the foreplay there.

Once you move to the bedroom, this is where you can start the in-depth foreplay, and move onto the heavy making out, and heavy petting. Start out slow, and gently. Do not move too fast, as you want to make the moment last. Slowly move from heavy petting to oral.

Once you both reach your first orgasm, this is when to start the actual sex part begins. If your spouse is male, and has a hard time getting it up after an orgasm, there is a trick to make him orgasm without ejaculating, as ejaculation is what releases all the hormones.

To do this, he has to be vocal about how close he is, and you have to find the right spot. Right behind his testicles, where they meet the perineum (area that connects the penis to the rectum) , is a hard spot about the size of a nickel. Right as he is about to ejaculate, you have to press hard on that spot, rubbing in circular motions. This will stop the ejaculation process, while still allowing him to feel the pleasure of an orgasm. It takes a few times to get this down, as you have to find the PC muscle and hit it at just the right time while continuing to stimulate him, but once you get it down, he can have multiple orgasms with no refractory time.

It is a lot easier for a female to have multiple orgasms if she is truly mentally present. For a female to have multiple orgasms though, or for her to even achieve one, she has to focus on how the sex feels. Ladies, you can't think about the milk in the fridge, and wonder if it is going to expire soon. You can't worry about if someone is going to hear you. You have to be selfish. Ask for what you want, and let yourself be free to feel the great feelings of sex. Don't try to put on an act, and don't worry about impressing your partner. I can assure you that seeing you enjoy yourself will be sexy enough for them. Just enjoy yourself in the raw moment.

A lot of experts say to fake it until you make it. This is great in theory, except you get so focused on faking it that you will never make it. You have to let it happen naturally. Otherwise you will be left disappointed every time.

Sex Positions

I bet right now you are trying to think of all the sex positions you can. Of course there is the standard ones such as missionary, doggy style, and cowgirl, but there are a few more that you should be aware of, and these ones are great sex positions to rock your world.

- The Cat: This position is great for allowing a female to achieve orgasm. It provides both penetration and clitoral stimulation. It is set up like the missionary, female on bottom, male on top. However, the males chest is above the females shoulders, and the females hips are raised. The male should grind rather than thrust for optimal pleasure.
- Waterfall: This is great for male orgasm. The setup is like the cowgirl, but the male hangs off of the bed with his head touching the floor, and his pelvis on the bed. Be careful not to be to rough with this position to avoid spinal injury.
- The Hot Seat: This is another good one for female orgasm, and as a plus, it puts her in control. Sit on a chair, or the edge of the bed, with your feet on the floor. Have her sit on your lap, and slide yourself into her. She can control

the angle and depth by leaning forward, or arching her back. You can also add variations of this by sitting on a washer or dryer on the highest agitation cycle, or on the staircase.

- Reverse Cowgirl: This is good for both partners to orgasm. It is exactly what the title states, the cowgirl with the female the opposite way.

- Pole Position: This one offers a great view for the guys, and great stimulation for the female. The male should lay on his back with one leg bent while the other is out straight. The female should straddle the raised leg, and slide onto the male's penis. The female gets penetration stimulation from the penis, and clitoral stimulation from the raised thigh.

- The Lap Dance: This one is great for intimacy. The male sits on the edge of the bed, and the female straddles him face to face. This is great for making out while having sex.

- The Anvil: This one is a very pleasurable technique. The female lies on her back, and the male kneels between her legs, resting the calves on his shoulders. This angle allows for deep penetration, and g-spot stimulation.

Those are some of the sex positions that will rock your worlds. Try out as many as you would like, and if you want you can even try to make up your own, or look up more online.

What is a Sex List

A sex list is literally what it says. A list of sex positions. You fill it up with positions you would like to try, along with styles you would like to try. BDSM, Pegging, Three-ways, etc. Don't be afraid that your partner will think you are weird, he or she probably has some weird stuff on their list as well.

Agree to a time line to finish your list by. This could be in days, weeks, or even years. I would suggest that you stretch it out for as long as possible, that way you have something to look forward to.

How to Make a Sex List

It is fairly simple. Look through all the kinds of sex positions, and sex styles you would like to try, and then write them down on the list. You and your partner should be open-minded to everything the other puts down, and you should vow to at least try everything each other has on their list at least once.

If there is something that you absolutely do not want to do, and can give a valid reason as to why, rather than "it just seems weird" then your partner should scratch it off the list. You should do the same for them if it is something they cannot do.

Sex is essential in a marriage, but not just plain sex. Sex that brings you closer together as you try new things and branch out. Sex is needed to procreate, and to ignite passion in your marriage.

Why this Key is Important

This key allows you to tap into your wild side, and be free with the person you most love. They get to see a side of you that no one else has, and that will allow you to build up a passion you have never felt before. By unlocking the beasts inside of yourselves, you can really connect with your partner.

CHAPTER 6

SECRET KEY #5

Find a Common Interest.

It is true what they say. People that play together stay together. This key unlocks the part of your brain that forms strong bonds with people, and this is necessary to unlock so that you can truly feel at home with the one you love. You need to form a bond that you have never experienced with anyone else in order to be truly happy with your partner. This will keep you in love with them for the rest of your lives.

While it may have been a common interest that brought you together, you probably have more different hobbies than you have hobbies together. You need common interests so that you have things to do together when you get alone time, and you don't spend that time in a constant barrage of "what do you want to do?" "I don't know, what do you want to do?" back and forth. This is almost as bad as trying to figure out where you want to go when you go out to eat.

So to avoid the boredom in each other's company, you should go explore some things together, and find some things that you enjoy doing together. There are many things you can do to find out what you like.

- Join a book club: If both you and your partner love to read, maybe a book club could be just what you need. You can discuss the meeting at home, and trade insight on the book you are reading. You can find time to read books together, and even read excerpts from the book out loud to your children. With a book club, you also get to meet other people with similar interests.
- Take Dance Classes: This is something to do to discover if either of you like dancing. It is always good to know a few basic dances anyhow. When taking dance classes remember,

it will take you a bit to learn if you like them or not, because you won't get the dances the first day.

- Go Hiking: Hiking is a great form of exercise, and a great way to bond with your partner. You can go hiking on a trail, and look at all sorts of scenery, and learn about nature, which is one of the most beautiful things in the world. The serenity will give you both peace of mind, and the exercise will keep you fit.
- Take a Shop Class: Learn about wood work or metal work. It is always wonderful to be able to create a work of art with your partner, and it is even better when it is functional.

There are many other things you can try to find a common interest. Try a new one every month until you find one that works for you. Because when you have something to talk about, then everything else flows easily after.

Go On Adventures

These adventures do not have to cost a lot of money. They just have to be something out of your usual routine. Go to your local park, and enjoy the scenery. Visit your local zoo, and see all the animals that are there. Go to the lake and go fishing or boating. It doesn't have to cost a lot, it just has to make a difference.

The best thing is, you can take your kids if you have them on these adventures. You can be together as a family, and teach your children new things. It is amazing the impact it has on your life, how much difference an afternoon out makes.

This next scenario will show you just how much different things can be before and after an adventure.

Scenario

Alice and Walker had been fighting a lot recently.

Literally all the time. Alice had recently found out that Walker had cheated on her with her ex best friend. She was furious, but didn't want to leave because she loved Walker, and they had three children together. She didn't want to split her family up.

So for the past two months of her life, she has been living in a miserable hell. Walker tried to act like nothing had happened, and didn't even try to apologize for hurting her like he did. He merely admitted that he made a mistake and it won't happen again, and left it at that. However, Alice's trust for him was completely shattered, and her heart was broken. That pain turned into anger most of the time, and Alice started fights over little things, or got irrationally angry. These fights could start at the drop of a hat, and last for hours. It was hell on Earth in that household. Till one day, their oldest daughter came out into the living room and said four words that changed their perspective.

"I hate living here" Macy said with tears in her eyes

"Oh baby girl, what's wrong?" Alicia asked

"Ever since Daddy hurt you, all you two do is fight. I wish Daddy would just leave. I hate seeing you unhappy Mommy."

"Don't you love me anymore, Mace?" Walker asked

"Of course I love you Daddy. You just hurt Mommy, and you should be punished. When it happens on TV, the mom kicks the dad out, and the dad only gets to visit. It teaches him a good lesson."

"Oh, Macy. That is TV. In real life, it isn't that easy. I love your father very much, and do not want him to leave. Things are just rough right now. My heart has an injury on it, like when you scrape your knee. And it is going to hurt until it heals. I know I shouldn't be so crabby, it is just hard sometimes." Alice explained.

"Alice, Macy, go get the other two, and pack a picnic

lunch. I have an idea." Walter suddenly said.

"Where are we going?' Alice asked

"It's a surprise."

Twenty minutes later, Walker, Alice, and the kids pulled into a beautiful field with a large pond. The sun on the water was amazing, and there were ducks and geese resting on the water. Armed with fishing poles, bait, bread crumbs, and a picnic basket filled with goodies, the family set out towards the pond.

"Oh my goodness. The spot where we had out first date, and you taught me how to fish!" Alice exclaimed.

"I figured we needed to go back to where it all began, to see how far we have come. Six years, and three beautiful children later." Walker stated, with tears in his eyes, as he watched his kids feed the ducks and geese. "I can't believe that Mace wants me gone. I really screwed up this time."

This was the closest that Walker had come to apologizing for his actions, and Alice felt her heart swell, as she saw for the first time, the regret on his face when he realized what he had done did indeed have some severe implications.

Throughout the day, Walker and Alice rekindled their flame as they taught their kids how to fish, went swimming in the pond, had a picnic on the dock, and lay back that evening and watched the sunset. For the first time in two months, their day was filled with laughter, rather than tears and yelling.

"I'm so sorry, Alice. I know I have never said it, I just couldn't bring myself to admit that my choice had any real effect on you. Even though I saw you hurting every day, it was easier to blame you than to admit I was the one with the problem. I am so sorry. Please, please, please forgive me." Walker apologized.

"Walker that is the first time you have said you are

sorry about this whole thing. That's is what I needed to hear. Yes I forgive you. I love you with all my heart. Can you forgive me for picking useless fights?"

"Alice, without those useless fights, I could have lost you and the kids. Those fights were you fighting for us, and I could never be mad at you for that." Walker pulled her up, and put their song playing on his phone, and he danced with her, as their children watched. Alice's heart swelled as she remembered this was the song they danced too on their very first date, in that very same spot.

"I knew then that you were the only one for me, and though I messed up and almost forgot that fact, I am even more sure now."

For the first time since she found out about the infidelity, Alice kissed him. Not a peck on the lips kind of kiss. She gave him one of those every day when he left for work. A deep, passionate kiss, filled with love and desire.

Once the kiss ended, Walker got down on one knee and pulled out her engagement ring, which she had taken off the day she learned of his transgressions.

"I know I messed up, and I want to do it better this time around. Alice, I love you with all of my heart. I never want to hurt you like that again. I have truly learned my lesson, and I want to have another chance to become the man you deserve in your life. Will you marry me?"

"Yes." Alice whispered, tears falling down her cheeks. In that moment she was the happiest she had been in months.

Their children cheered, and were ecstatic to see their parents happy again. They finished the night out with stargazing, and a healing family.

Discussion

Alice and Walker's marriage was severely on the rocks after Walker's infidelity was brought to life. It seemed like things would never get better, but after a wake-up call, and a little family adventure, Alice and Walker were on the path to setting things right again. It won't be perfect over night, but with a little work, a rocky marriage can be fixed.

Those are the five secret keys to a successful, passionate, and intimate relationship. Read on for more info on tips and tricks to know what to expect, and if your marriage is just on the rocks, or if it is dangerous.

Why You Need This Key

To truly be in love with someone, you need to

experience something together, that you haven't with anyone else. Finding a common interest or going on adventures will unlock that experience for you so that you can truly feel each other deep down in your souls.

CHAPTER 7

EXTRA HELP FOR THOSE IN A VULNERABLE PLACE

Is it Rocky? Or Dangerous?

I included this chapter to address a common phenomenon that I realized is commonly overlooked by most. That is how to recognize a rocky marriage versus a potentially abusive and dangerous one. It is vital that you understand the difference so that you are able to discern a healthy versus a toxic marriage. Healthy marriages can be fixed. Toxic marriages will need a large clean-up crew to fix the massive oil-spill. And as we know, the existing toxicity has already begun destroying the beauty that it had infected. Be alert to the warning signs please. Here we go.

A rocky marriage can be fixed with a little understanding. If you are fighting over simple things that can be changed but you want some expert advice by a health professional to breathe new insights into the source of the problems between you and your spouse, seeing a marriage counselor might be an excellent idea. The counselor can help you and your spouse delve deeper into the underlying issues of the marriage and to work towards a healthy resolution.

However, if your partner is always picking fights based on things you can't change, like your appearance, your voice, your shoe size, or even how you breathe. Say What? Well if they are constantly make you feel insecure, it could be indication that there is some deeper issues with the relationship that might not be so easily solved. Now if it gets violent, that's when you NEED help. Also i might classify some of the above mentions as abuse. Abuse you say? Yes abuse.

Abuse isn't always physical, though that is a part of it. Abuse can take the form where they make you feel so low about yourself that you want to end it all to make your life easier. Or if they make you feel trapped in your marriage, and tell you they are the only person who will ever love you, and that you should be grateful they put up with you. Generally this is the behavior of a narcissist. Do not allow this to continue. Tell them how they make you feel, and if they are willing to try to change, it is okay to give them one more chance, as long as they actively get professional help. However, if they continue to belittle your feelings and you realize they can never change, it is time to think long and hard whether you would want to be spending the rest of your life with such a person.

Get a second opinion from your friends and loved ones. Make an informed decision and act on it fast. I firmly believe that this type of treatment is absolutely unacceptable, unhealthy for the abused, and belongs nowhere in a marriage.

Remember, if they hit you. They will more than likely do it again. This goes for both men and women. Either gender can be the victim, either gender can be the perpetrator. No matter your gender, you should never feel bad about getting help. There are many different resources out there you can reach out to. The best one is http://www.ncadv.org/learn-more/get-help. It gives you a list of places that will help you out, and gives you tips for staying safe.

Be safe, and remember, just because you say "I do" does not mean that you have to stay with your abuser.

Relationship Breakthrough

(Bonus)

Achieve Massive Success In Your Relationship That Others Would Kill For

J. S. PARKER

CONTENTS

1	Breakthrough With Guys	
2	Chapter 1: Why Do You Need These Secret Keys for A Relationship Breakthrough?	86
3	Chapter 2: Secret Key 1 - Desire	89
4	Chapter 3: Secret Key 2 - Feeling of Security	105
5	Chapter 4: Secret Key 3 - Respect and Compassion	111
6	Chapter 5: Secret Key 4 - Confidence	122
7	Chapter 6: Secret Key 5 – Give and Take the Lead	128
8	Breakthrough With Girls	125
9	Chapter 1: What Do You Want?	128
10	Chapter 2: Secret Key 1 – Open, Honest, Consistent Communication	132
11	Chapter 3: Secret Key 2 – Equality and Respect	135
12	Chapter 4: Secret Key 3 – Acceptance for Who They Are	140
13	Chapter 5: Secret Key 4 – The Pedestal	151
14	Chapter 6: Secret Key 5 – Make Her Smile	157
15	Chapter 7: Special Bonus Tips	164

16 Conclusion

CHAPTER 1

WHAT ARE THESE SECRET KEYS TO A RELATIONSHIP BREAKTHROUGH?

Have you ever wondered why so many people fail in their relationship with men, whether as friends or more than that? Wondered why so many couples break up, even though it seemed like they would be together forever? Do you have a hard time connecting with men enough to take your relationship to the highest level possible? Many people do, and that is because they do not know about these secret keys for a breakthrough.

It is essential to know what men want and need, otherwise, you will not be able to know him as well as you wish you could, and the distance will make it hard to connect. A connection is important when in a relationship, as it is what determines the amount of passion you have years down the road. A weak connection makes for weak passion and limited intimacy once the honeymoon phase is over.

If you do not have passion and intimacy in a marriage, this can be a major problem, as they are what keep the love alive, and the marriage interesting. Without any interest in your marriage, it can cause many problems, including divorce, and infidelity.

So to avoid these issues you must learn about the secret keys, for without them you will be destined to have an average relationship, rather than a superb relationship. Which an average one can last forever, but a superb relationship will most definitely last forever.

Only about twenty percent of people know about these keys to a man's heart. They are the couples that you see that are eighty years old and still acting like young lovers. They are the couples that everyone aspires to be. These people are the happiest couples alive because they learned the secret keys to marriage, and to unlock their man's heart.

Why it is Pertinent to Know these Keys

These keys are the basis of obtaining a strong and intimate relationship. Almost everyone's goal in life is to get married, and have that marriage last forever. They want to be the couple that everyone looks up to, and that everyone comes to for advice.

That is where these keys come in. They are designed to help you achieve that level of a relationship in your life. These are from a man's perspective, to help you understand more what they really want. Not what women say they want.

A man's heart is unique. It is unlike a woman's heart in many ways, and should be treated as such. You should want to know exactly how to open his heart to show you exactly how he wants to be loved.

Men are also stubborn at times. You may have already won his heart, but he has put up walls to try to prevent himself from falling. You have to break through these walls as well, which if you use these keys, should be easier than just whacking away at it with charm. Read on to find these keys.

Chapter 2:

Secret Key #1

Desire

Men do not say this aloud, which is why this key is such a big secret, but men love romance. They want their partners to put in a little romantic effort as well. This key is important, as without it, a man cannot be sure if you are really down for him or not. If he doesn't feel like you desire him, he will not completely open up to you. Very few couples realize how important this is, and that is why often times, you see relationships fizzle out so fast. Follow this key to strengthen your bond with the male species.

Romance

Describe your most romantic fantasy. Is it elaborate? Or simple? Either way, you most likely still have one. So does he. Men are romantic creatures by nature, but they also like to be romanced. Take him out to dinner, and pick up the check. Take him out to the movies, and pay for him. Return the favor he probably often shows you quite frequently.

It doesn't even have to be that expensive either. When he has a long day at work, surprise him with his favorite dinner served by candlelight. In his day off, pack a picnic lunch, and drive to his favorite spot and enjoy a picnic. It doesn't have to always be fancy, you just need to put in as much effort into showing him you want him, as he does for you.

It is about feeling wanted, and loved. If you aren't putting in an effort to show him how much you care, how is he going to know that you are going to be there in the long run? He will feel like you are only there for what he can do for you, not what you can do together, and he will begin to feel used. Value a man. Don't expect to get treated like royalty if you are only going to treat him like a peasant.

To understand more about being romantic for a guy, this scenario will help you to understand more, that it isn't always about the big things, sometimes even the smallest gesture means the world to a guy.

Scenario

James looked over at his girlfriend, and wondered if she truly loved him. She said it all the time, but how did he know for sure? Was she just fronting to get his money or was she truly his ride or die chick? How could he be sure that she really loved him?

"Babe?" He called over to MaryBeth

"Yes, baby?" She replied

"Answer three questions for me. What is my favorite color? What was my favorite memory as a child? What is my favorite food?" James needed to know if she loved him as much as he loved her. He knew that her favorite color was purple, because it reminded her of the twilight hours when everything is quiet and still. He knew that her favorite childhood memory was when her dad took some free bikes and pieced them together to make her very first bike because they were too poor to buy a new one. He knew that her favorite food was Italian, and that it only became so when she met him, because he was Italian, and showed her how real cuisine was created, rather than restaurants that order frozen food and heat it up in a microwave. He wanted to see if she knew the answers to those questions.

"You don't have a favorite color, per say. You are color blind. You say that your favorite color would be emerald green because that is the color I told you my eyes were. Your favorite childhood memory was when you and your brother climbed the big oak tree in your backyard together, and talked about life and what your plans were for your futures. You said that was the first time you two had really ever bonded, and that was when you realized you wanted to be a real estate investor. You were nine. Your favorite food is Chinese, because it reminds you of when your mother used to take you to a Chinese restaurant every Friday for mother-son bonding time. The last time you did that with her was two days before she died. You used to dislike Chinese food, but went because she loved it, but after she died, the memories made you love it." She answered. "Now tell me. What is this about?"

"I was wondering if you loved me. No girl has ever paid enough attention to me, and focused mainly on my wallet. You answered every question perfectly. The first one to ever do so. I love you so much."

"How could you doubt I love you, James? I may not have a lot of money, but I try to show you every day that I love you. You should think about that, rather than focusing on little questions that anyone who pays attention to you could answer." MaryBeth replied, slightly offended that he felt she didn't love him.

As she walked out of the room, James sat and thought about what she said. He thought back over the course of their relationship, and thought about all the things she did for him regularly.

She cooks me dinner on a regular basis. When I have had a hard day, she rubs my back. Even though she is on her feet for over eight hours a day, and mine is just stress of a tenant not wanting to pay rent. She shows up on my longer days with my favorite meal, and we eat it together before we have to go back to work. For no reason at all, she told me to get in the car, and we drove to our favorite spot with some fast food, and ate while watching the trains pull into the station.

She always tells me she loves me before she goes to bed, even if she is angry with me. She never fails to ask me how my day was, and truly listen to the answer. Even though sometimes I tune her out when she talks about hers. I don't know what her favorite song is, or when her first heartbreak happened, but she sure as hell know mine. What have I done for her? I know the answer to three questions that anyone with half a brain could answer, and I buy her stuff. I take her out to fancy dinners, and spend money on her but that is about it, and yet she never questions my love for her. I want to marry this woman. She is my everything. She has a piece of me that no one else ever will. She truly has my heart.

James walked back into the bedroom, where he found MaryBeth crying. He sat beside her, and began to rub her back.

"I'm sorry. I am so sorry I ever doubted your love for me. I know I could say that every other girlfriend has only wanted my money, and it broke me, but in truth; I am just an ass. I love you, MaryBeth. I want to marry you someday. Not today, we still have a lot of things to work through, but if you forgive me, I promise that one day you will have an engagement ring on your finger." James said, pulling out a little ring and sliding it on her ring finger. "Do you accept my promise?"

"Yes. I forgive you as well." MaryBeth said, beaming with happiness while her eyes were still brimming with tears.

Discussion

James didn't realize until it was brought to his attention, all the little things that MaryBeth does for him to show her love. Sometimes you do have to give him a little wake up call to show him that you do play the romance card on a regular basis. Maybe do a big gesture here and there to really show him you care. But sometimes it just takes you telling him to think that gets his brain in gear. Be romantic, and even if he doesn't realize it at first, he will start to see all the little things you do for him, even when he doesn't notice you doing them.

Desire

You have to ignite a white-hot passion in him that makes him want to take you right here and right now almost any where you go. This desire is what fuels the passion in your relationship. If there is no passion, things get stale, and that is when people drift apart the most. If the bedroom isn't rocking, you better get packing, because you need a good sex life, and desire filled relationship to last for a long time.

How do you ignite this desire in him? It is simple. You have to desire him as well. Men are easily enticed, if you are willing to tap into your animalistic nature. You have to want to make him desire you, so that means you will have to be pro-active in your sexuality, and prove your prowess in the bedroom, along with outside the bedroom.

How is this done exactly? Ditch the missionary position. This is the bane of all sexual existence. There are so many more positions out there, where you don't have to lie there like a lifeless doll and take what he is giving you. (Ditch standard doggy style for gay couples. This is the missionary in the gay world.) Look up new positions and try them for yourselves. Try different styles. There are some that can spice up the bedroom if you are both willing to try it.

- BDSM: This is a type of sexual style that requires one partner to be dominant, and one partner to be submissive. Start out slow. Don't go "Fifty Shades of Grey" level the first day. Ease into it. Find out the limitations your bodies can handle, how tight you like the collars and ties, what you absolutely do not like, and so on and so forth. Knowing what you like is important, as if you don't like it, the experience will not be fun. Both of you have to be vocal if you want to know what each other likes and don't like. Also, come up with a safe word to use, so in the heat of the moment, you don't hurt yourselves.

- Roleplay: This is one for when you want to experience what it is like to have sex with someone different, yet still wanting that sex to be with your partner. You get little costumes, and you dress up as someone else. While dressed up as another person, you literally become that person. You are not yourself, you are a whole other person. This could mean you have your guy become the cable guy, or you become his secretary. There are many other people you can take on the role of, such as famous people, or make up your own personas. If you do not feel comfortable with role play, but are still intrigued by it, try it on a small scale.

Have him be a fake person you make up, and vice versa. This will get you more comfortable with the idea, so you can more enjoy it.

- Making a Home Video: This can be a very good bonding experience in the bedroom, as you can watch back the video you make, and see how much you were enjoying the sex. Once you both realize how good things are in the bedroom, you will never want to leave. Relax and enjoy it, though. Don't try to put on a show just because you are being filmed. You aren't a porn star, and neither is he. Just enjoy it. You can also see what positions work for you, and what doesn't when you play the video back. These videos should never be put on the internet, or used for any other reason than your viewing pleasure. If handled correctly, they can make for great material to get you in the mood as well.

- Watch Porn Together: This can give you an idea on positions to try, and also get you in the mood to do the deed. Find a video that you both like, and settle in. You can also try a bit of self stimulation while watching the video, but be careful not to distract yourself, or your partner from the video itself. The whole point is to learn new positions and bond. Remember though, porn is an act. Do not expect to have super explosive orgasms the first time you try a position. You most likely will have to practice a few times for it to even feel good.

There are many ways to spark up some interest in the bedroom, but how do you make him want to do these things? How do you spark the carnal desire in him? How do you show him you want him so bad it makes your stomach do flips? There are a few ways that are fool proof.

- Send Him Little Notes: You can leave sticky notes all over the house for him, in his car, in his lunchbox if he has one. You can also text him all the things you would like to do to him. Tell him that you aren't wearing any underwear or something like that. Give him something to want later that night.

- Tease Him: Kiss him seductively in the hall way and then keep moving along. Rub your rear against his junk, and then walk away. Play footsie with him when you eat dinner. Make him desire you, turn him on, but then leave him hanging. At the end of the night he will want you so bad, he will do anything to have you.

- Be Playful: Sometimes the biggest turn on is when you act like a kid. Being free-spirited can be the biggest turn on for guys, because they like knowing you are happy and having fun. Tickle him, and then make him chase you to the bedroom and tackle you on the bed. Play wrestle a little bit, and watch the playing turn into sex real fast. Sometimes the best foreplay, is to simply play.

You have to create a white-hot desire in the pit of his stomach, one that makes him crave you when you are away, and not want to leave your side when you are near. You have to make him think about you constantly, to the point where he doesn't even want you to go to the restroom because that means being away from you for too long.

This desire will unlock the part of his heart that makes him want to commit. He won't want to leave, because he is too devoted to you, and he loves you way too much to walk away from everything you have together. You have to keep this desire alive, and strong, to keep the relationship strong and healthy.

Here is a scenario that should help you get a mental picture of what that desire looks like. Caution. This one is mildly graphic, but if you are an adult reading this, as the disclaimer warns, you have probably read much worse.

Scenario

He wanted her. He wanted her more than he has ever wanted anyone. The way she teased him drove him insane. It was like she took pleasure in keeping him aroused to the point of pain. She would pay for it, when she finally let him have her. These thoughts swirled around Mason's brain, and left him winded. He thought back to when they first met.

Lacy wasn't like a lot of girls. That is what attracted Mason to her. He was tired of girls throwing themselves at him. He was tired of girls who had nothing more to offer than a loose vagina, and some amateur head. These women bored Mason, so he never kept them around much longer than a night. Lacy, however, showed very little interest in Mason when they first met. She looked him up and down, offered her hand in a professional manner, and said it was nice to meet him. Like she was at a job interview. She didn't blush, or swoon, or make any indication that she found Mason attractive. He had to have her. She was exactly what he wanted. A challenging woman.

He became more and more infatuated with her as the night drew on, and he listened to her talk, and engaged in conversation with her. She was Harvard educated, and it showed. She wasn't haughty or anything, really she was very humble, but when she spoke her words were eloquent and well thought out. She didn't use 'like' in between every word, as most girls tend to do. Instead, every word out of her mouth was carefully planted like she was speaking a puzzle.

She turned him on. Plain, and simple. He had to have a date with her.

"Excuse me, Lacy? I am enamored by your eloquence, and would love to talk to you more, one-on-one. Would you care to have a cup of coffee with me after this party is over?" Mason asked

"Why don't we leave right now? I feel I am boring everyone else." Lacy said

"I highly doubt you are boring anyone, but if you wish, I would love to go at once."

They left the club, and walked down the street to a little coffee shop that was open twenty four hours a day. This was one of Mason's spots to think, and he wanted Lacy to experience it as well. When they walked in, he could tell that she was star-struck with the place. It wasn't well known, but it was cozy. He offered to buy her coffee, but she refused, stating that she was glad to have an excuse to leave the club.

"I hope you don't think that I am like other girls, Mason." Lacy said as soon as the found a cozy nook to sit down.

"I beg you are pardon?" Mason nearly choked on his latte

"I don't put out on the first date. You have to win my heart. You can't just bring me to a quaint little coffee shop, and expect me to sleep with you tonight." Lacy was blunt with what she spoke, there was no beating around the bush.

"Of course I don't think you are like other girls. In fact, I have never brought a woman here before."

As if on cue, the shop owner came out then to greet Mason.

"Mason, my old friend. Are you enjoying your evening? Oh! You have a lady with you! Forgive me for interrupting, I have never seen this before. Enjoy yourselves." The shop owner ducked back into his office with a bright red face.

"Well I guess I don't need to ask you to prove that you have never brought a woman here."

They sat and talked the night away. In the wee hours of the morning, Mason drove Lacy home, as her friends had already left the club.

"Lacy, can I see you again?" Mason asked, as she stepped out of the car.

"I would like that very much."

Three months later, Lacy practically lived with him. They often slept in the same bed. And he still had not been able to make love to her. That is what he wanted. He didn't want to just have sex with her, he wanted to make love to her.

"What is on your mind, Mace?" Lacy asked, sitting on his lap.

"I want you, Lacy. More than I have ever wanted anyone. I love you. I truly love you. I want to make passionate love to you, in a way no man ever has. I want to give you the world, if you will let me. You are the one I want. Forever."

"Mason, that is what I have been wanting to hear since we met. Tonight you will finally get what you want. Me."

That night was the most mind blowing night of

Mason's life. Lacy felt perfect for him. They didn't leave the bedroom for hours. Everything was perfect.

Flash forward two years later, and Lacy still teased him. He still wanted her as much as he did from day one. He couldn't imagine life with any other woman, as she was the only one who lit such a desire in him.

Discussion

Lacy made Mason desire her, by not always being readily available. She let him know she was into him, but she did not give up everything from the beginning, and even after she gave it all up, she still kept that playfulness up in the relationship, making him want her bad enough to always desire her.

This is what you have to do in a relationship. You have to keep your partner interested in you. Don't think that just because you have been together for a long time, that means you have to act like an old couple. Be playful. Show each other how much you care.

Chapter 3:

Secret Key #2

Make Him Feel Safe

Men will never admit that they need to feel safe in a relationship. This key is a secret, because society makes men feel that they have to be macho all the time. This is the furthest from the truth, and you should not believe this, as everyone needs to feel safe. Not just physically, but emotionally.

Couples that know this often have less fights, and less time spent angry at each other. Fights and arguments do not stem from someone doing something that you don't agree with, they stem from being afraid that they are going to leave you. You get angry because you don't feel safe, and you are scared you are going to be left alone, so you throw up a wall. Men do the same thing as everyone else. Only they will never admit that is why they have a wall up.

You have to make him want to take all of his walls down and be open with you. Make him feel like you want to know everything about him. Not just where he grew up, what his favorite color is, and what music does he like. Ask him if he ever sucked his thumb, did he have a teddy bear or a blankie? What was his favorite television show growing up? Has he ever been in trouble? What are his aspirations, and fears? Ask him about his nightmares. Do not be satisfied with one word answers. Give him information about you every time he divulges something about himself.

Emotional Safety

You have to be his safety net as he is free-falling into

love with you, just as he has to be yours. You have to catch each other, and you can't fall if you don't trust the other person with your heart. Be open always. You can't expect him to open up to you when you won't open up to him. It is a give and take relationship, when you want to unlock the part of his heart he holds dearest to him.

To make him feel emotionally safe, you have to let him know that you won't let him down. This often means listening to him talk about things you aren't necessarily interested in.

A man has to be able to cry around you to feel truly and completely safe in a relationship. Sometimes you have to assure him that it is okay to cry. Hold him when you see him having a weak moment, and let him know that sometimes even the strongest mountain breaks down. If he can't cry around you, he won't be truly open to you. Men are at their most vulnerable moments in life when they break down in front of someone, because they are bred to believe that crying means you are weak. So if a man finally cries in front of you, you have won his heart.

Here is a scenario of how to know if you make him feel emotionally safe.

Scenario

Josh loved his boyfriend very much, but he felt as if Alex was still closed off. Josh was definitely the more feminine of the two, so he was very open with Alex. Alex however, often changed the subject when it came to his past. Josh knew that Alex loved him, he just wasn't ready to completely open up. Josh was understanding, and never pushed, but still let his love know that he was there for him.

One day, Alex came home in a horrible mood. Josh didn't know what was wrong, but he ran up and hugged Alex anyway.

"Oh, baby, I can just tell you had a horrible day. Would

you like to talk about it?" Josh asked.

"Actually I would like that very much, babe." Alex said with a tight throat.

"Come sit down darling, let me make you your favorite tea while you compose your thoughts."

Josh hurried off to the kitchen, while Alex sat down on the couch, looking lost and forlorn. Josh's hear broke just looking at how sad his love looked. After the tea finished brewing, Josh hurried back into the living room, and handed Alex his tea, made just the way he liked it.

"What happened love?" Josh asked gently.

"I guess there is no sense in beating around the bush. My brother is dead. He was shot in the head last night in a drug deal gone wrong." Alex said

"I am so sorry love. I didn't know you had a brother, but I am heartbroken for you nonetheless." Josh said, wrapping his arms around Alex.

"I didn't talk about him much because I was ashamed

of him. He was a drug addict. He was always asking when he could meet you, and I always made excuses. I feel horrible now, because he was the only one who supported me when I came out as gay. My parents kicked me out, and he gave me a place to stay. He was the only family I had, and I judged him for something he had about as much control over as I do being gay." Alex broke down in tears.

Josh sat there and held Alex, his heart breaking for him, as it also beamed with love, because Alex was finally opening up to him. He was sad that Alex's only true family was dead, but happy that Alex trusted him enough to tell him everything. His heart swelled with love for the man in his arms crying his eyes out.

Discussion

Alex was very closed off when it came to talking about his past, because it hurt to much to talk about, and he didn't want to cry in front of Josh, and Josh felt distanced from Alex due to his wall he threw up. Once

Alex finally started talking about himself, Josh knew that Alex truly loved him, and that he trusted him finally. This gave Josh a happy feeling, even in the midst of a sad time, which allowed him to truly comfort Alex in his moment of need.

Why Do You Need This Key Again?

This key is essential in opening up an intense bond between you and your partner. When you feel comfortable enough to be completely open with each other, you learn more about the other than you could ever imagine. This is important, because to truly love someone, you have to truly know them. Once you truly know everything about someone, loving them becomes a whole lot easier.

Chapter 4:

Secret Key #3

Respect and Compassion

What is the one thing that anyone wants more than anything in the world? That is right, respect. Respect is rated the number one thing that a person wants in life. It is even more of a priority than love, because you can't have love if you don't have respect.

Respect is what makes the world go round. Think

Aretha Franklin. R-E-S-P-E-C-T. This song is about how just a little respect can make a world of difference. You have to respect your partner not only as your partner, but as a human being as well. You can't expect them to be perfect, and you have to respect that sometimes they have to make mistakes.

This is where compassion comes in. When your partner makes a mistake, it is always important to show them compassion and understanding. This way they know that you care enough to help them make it through the mistakes they have made.

Why is this a Secret Key?

Most people do not know that men need more respect and compassion in the relationship. Men are often more insecure then women, they are just better at hiding it. Respect and compassion assure him that you love him and care about him, and that he is good enough for you. If he feels that he is worthy of you, he will become the most devoted person you have ever met. This key unlocks the section in his heart tied to fidelity. If he feels worthy of you, he will do anything to stay there. If he does not feel worthy of you, he will look for someone who makes him feel worthy.

EGO

This all boils down to ego. A man's ego is a powerful thing. Sometimes, if not treated properly, he can become borderline narcissistic. If he feels that he is not getting the respect he deserves, he will look to get it in any way he can. This is where a lot of severe relationship problems stem from. Emotional abuse, physical abuse, infidelity. This is all a problem created when a man is beaten down. Not necessarily by you, but by the world. This is what causes people to split up, and can ruin what seemed to be a perfect relationship.

Men aren't always aware of their ego issues, so they

can't tell you what they need. That is not to excuse a man who becomes abusive or a cheater, or even to say that a man is helpless. They know right from wrong, they just don't realize what is causing them to do wrong. If he is abusive or a cheater, then you should leave. No questions asked. Leave. However, if he is just being angry for no reason, maybe you aren't showing each other enough respect and compassion.

How to Show Him Respect

- Be there for him: If he has a gig, or something important, go with him. Even if you aren't interested. Being there for him, and respecting him enough to support him shows him how much you care. If he needs you to listen to him, do so. Let him rant on about something you don't care about, but pay attention. Just because you don't care doesn't give you a free pass to ignore him or tune him out.

- Respect His Privacy: Trust is a big thing in a relationship. Both parties need their privacy on some things, and breaking that privacy is saying that you don't trust your partner enough to give him space. A big thing that a lot of women do is go through his phone. If you can't trust him enough to leave his phone alone, you probably shouldn't be in a relationship. You also shouldn't snoop through his drawers or his personal things. Let him have his privacy, just as you want yours.

- Respect His Personal Space: You don't have to be together every free moment you both have. Sometimes, spending time apart when you have free time is a good thing. You can do your own thing, and don't have to worry about if the other person is having fun. Men need this personal space to unwind after a hard day. Women do as well, but we are focusing on men here. If he doesn't text you back immediately, he is probably in the shower or taking a nice hot bubble bath. It does NOT mean he is cheating on you. Let him have his space without worrying about him stepping out on you. If you trust and respect him, he most likely will not want to do anything to break that trust. But if you don't trust him, he might just give you a reason not to.

- Respect the Fact that He is Human: Men are not robots, and they are not slaves. He has needs, and he needs them tended to at times as well. You cannot expect him to wait on you hand and foot, yet not turn around to do the same for him. Also he will mess up. Don't hang it over his head for the rest of his life. Get through it, and then get over it.

Those are some ways that you can show that you respect him. Men are easy to please, and as they do not have the hormone fluxes that women do, it is more straightforward, but you still have to dig a little to find out his needs. He will give you what you need, if you respect him enough to let him.

Compassion

Compassion is important for when he is having a hard day or makes a mistake. You have to be willing to be compassionate towards someone to ever make a relationship work. Compassion is the difference between healing his heart and breaking it. If you are compassionate, he will trust you with things he doesn't trust anyone else with.

How to Be Compassionate

- Take Care of Him: If he is having a bad day, cook for him. Clean for him. Rub his back and cuddle him. I know this new-age mentality is that women are not a man's slave and that he can do for himself. That may be true, but sometimes you have to take care of him. In return, he will take care of you.

- Be Understanding: Men are human, and they will mess up. Don't overreact if he buys they wrong type of toilet paper, or the wrong grade of milk. They don't always get everything right. You have probably messed up sometimes as well. Did he freak out over the little things? Relax. If he isn't out killing people, or cheating on you, then discuss it calmly on why you prefer things a different way, and then make like Elsa and 'Let it Go'.

- Don't Ridicule Him: If he is not as advanced as you in some areas, do not make him feel bad for it. If you can read the best, and he can do math the best, combine your strengths. Don't make him feel like less of a person because he can't do what you can. Don't tell him he needs to get better. If he wants to, then help him, but don't tell him he has to.

- Listen to His Problems: The best thing you can ever do is just listen when he wants to talk. Not only will you learn some new things, but you will show him that you are invested in him, and by showing him a little compassion, you make him feel like he is important.

This scenario will show you how respect and compassion can help save a relationship.

Scenario

Rachel was worried about Rick. He had been acting distant lately, and was gone a lot. He always hid his phone and wouldn't let her touch it. Everyone said that he was probably cheating, but she trusted him to have a good reason for all of these things. She didn't want to be let down again by another man.

I will have a talk with him when he gets home tonight.

I will ask him why he has been acting this way.
Suddenly she heard a phone ring. She checked her pockets, but it wasn't hers. She investigated the sound, and found her boyfriend's phone behind the toilet. There was a strange number calling.

Should I answer it? No. I trust him. It is probably just a telemarketer, and his phone probably fell behind the toilet this morning, and he didn't grab it cause he was running late to work.

Rachel knew that Rick would be home in a few hours, so she busied herself with errands and cleaning the house up. Five o'clock rolled by, and Rick still wasn't home. She started to get worried, and with no way to contact him, she couldn't allay her fears. But she told herself to remain calm, and that he would show up. Finally, around seven o'clock, Rick came walking in the door. Rachel flung herself into his arms because she was so worried. Then she noticed that he didn't smell like the fiberglass mill, and he was surprisingly clean for being at work all day.

"Rick. We really need to talk." Rachel whispered, on the verge of tears.

"What's wrong?" Rick asked her

"I have been trusting of you, and I still trust you to tell me what is going on. I am trying not to assume you are cheating. However it is really hard to think of any other explanation why you have been coming home late, hiding your phone behind the toilet and getting strange calls. I didn't answer it by the way. Your clothes are too clean to be coming out of the fiberglass company, and they are the same clothes you walked out of here wearing. You don't smell like you normally do after work. Please just tell me what is going on." Rachel burst into tears.

"Oh Rach." Rick sighed, pulling her into his arms. "I got laid off a couple of weeks ago, and have been looking for a job ever since. That number was probably a job calling so I have to call back tomorrow.

I'm late because I have been doing odd jobs to continue making enough money to support us, so you don't have to. I wanted to tell you, I just didn't want you to worry."

"That is what this is all about? You knew I was cheated on several times by my last guy, and you leave me worrying that it is happening again? Babe, I would have understood if you had told me, and I would have supported you, and even got a job myself if need be. I love you, and I want you to tell me about your problems. Please don't hide something like this again."

"Oh Rachel, I love you so much, and I didn't realize how bad it looked. I am so sorry, and I promise to always tell you about these things from now on." Rick said, kissing Rachel passionately.

Discussion

Rachel could have jumped to conclusions and accused

Rick of cheating on her, thus making him angry for her not trusting him. However, she decided to ask him about it and listen to what he had to say. She was understanding when he told her what was going on, and let him know she wanted him to bring his troubles to her, even if it meant that he had to put some stress on her. She wanted to take on these problems together.

By being compassionate, and respecting him enough to trust him, she avoided what could have been a really big fight. Instead they were brought closer together, as they opened up with what was bothering them.

Why is this Key Important Again?

You have to respect each other to get anywhere in a relationship. Without respect you have nothing, and you can't truly love someone if you do not respect them. Compassion is needed to ensure that your relationship is not a miserable one. You have to respond with compassion to avoid having an argument blown out of proportion. People are not robots or dolls, they will mess up.

You have to use this key to unlock the part of a man's heart that trusts you. He doesn't open it up for just anyone. Most men do not trust half of the people they say are close to them. They could not be vulnerable to these people. You have to unlock that for yourself.

Chapter 5:

Secret Key #3

Be Confident

Men do not want to be with a woman who is always questioning if she is good enough for him. They want a woman who knows her worth. Men want to know they are with someone who feels valued. If you aren't confident, it makes his job of making you feel secure that much harder. He feels he always has to lift your self esteem, and that can be a hard job for anyone. Confidence is not always just knowing you are worthy of love, however. It is also taking care of yourself. Taking care of your personal hygiene and keeping yourself groomed. You do not have to be perfect, just put an effort into keeping yourself clean and well kept.

Most people don't realize that this is important in a relationship, and that is what makes it a secret key. It is important to use this to unlock his desires for you if you are looking to start a relationship with him, and you must remain confident and well kept to unlock his never waning desires for you.

Confidence

Everyone has their insecurities, there is no doubt about that. However it is important to not let your insecurities rule your life. You can have some things that make you not so sure about yourself, but you have to be able to work through them.

Confidence is important in any aspect of your life, but it is certainly important in relationships. Not only do you have to be confident in yourself, you have to be confident in your relationship as well. You can't expect a relationship to thrive if you don't have any confidence in it. You have to believe that it will succeed, and that you are good enough for it to succeed.

In this scenario, you will learn more about what poor confidence can do to a relationship.

Scenario

Blake was super insecure. He constantly doubted himself, and if he was good enough for his boyfriend Michael. Michael hated that Blake was so insecure, and wished he could see how gorgeous he was. It caused many fights, because Blake felt that he wasn't good enough and did everything in his power to make Michael see that. Which included picking fights for no reason at all.

I wish I was confident enough to make this relationship work. I am just not good enough for him.

He is perfect, and I am a fat lard. I really need to lose weight. I am so fat. Why does he stay with me? Can't he see I'm a disaster?

These are the thoughts that went through Blake's head daily. He couldn't ever get close to Michael, because he was scared that Michael would see that he was a disaster. He constantly had a wall up that Michael was trying to break down.

I'm exhausted. Blake never lets me in, and I'm am so tired of trying to break through the walls he puts up. I wish he could see how much he means to me. He is perfect just the way he is, if only he would stop worrying so much.

Michael was tired of always trying to boost Blake's self esteem, so with a heavy heart, he broke up with Blake.

"I told you I wasn't good enough!" Blake screamed, with tears in his eyes.

"You imbecile! That is the reason I am breaking up

with you! You don't feel like you are good enough for me, and I am tired of you ignoring every effort I make to try to show you otherwise! You are perfect just the way you are, and I wish I could have made you see that! I don't want to leave, but I can't keep breaking my heart when you won't let me into yours!" Michael yelled back.

"So you aren't breaking up with me because I'm not breaking up with you, you are merely breaking up with me because I feel like I am not?" Blake whispered

"Yes. I want nothing more than to be with you, but I have to think of my own emotional health as well."

"What if I promised to get help for my insecurities? Would you stay with me? I love you Michael, I just don't want to be hurt anymore. I want you to love me too."

"I do love you Blake, and if you actively get help, then yes, I will stay. But you have two weeks to show me you are trying." Michael said, embracing Blake.

Discussion

Blake's insecurities almost cost him the love of his life. He was so worried about Michael pushing him away, that he didn't realize he was the one doing the pushing. Blake was not confident in himself, and it was tiresome for Michael to always be the one to supply the confidence for the both of them. Michael felt like Blake couldn't truly love him, because he never let him in. It almost destroyed their relationship beyond repair.

If Blake had realized that Michael wanted to be with him for who he was, he would have avoided this whole scene, and been very happy. Let your confidence shine through. You may not feel confident, but fake it until you make it. If you seem confident, you will start to feel confident.

Take Care of Yourself

Men want women to be healthy. This does not mean that you have to eat organic food, and wear full face makeup every day of your life. Just shower regularly, and keep yourself groomed. If you are a slob, and unhygienic, most men will feel that is a sign of lack of confidence, and they will stay away from you. You have to make yourself appear to be ready for a relationship to find the right relationship. If you look like you don't care about yourself you are going to attract someone who doesn't care about you as well.

If you are in a relationship, and start letting yourself go, you will make your man feel like you don't care about the relationship as much as you used to. (This doesn't count if you have kids. Though you should still try to shower regularly) You should always want to keep your hygiene up regardless of your relationship status.

Why is this Key Important?

This key unlocks a man's desire for you. Human's

primal instinct is to mate, and men are really close to their primal instincts. He will be looking for a strong woman suitable for carrying his children, so that his offspring are strong and successful. By being confident, and taking care of yourself, you attract men that will value you, and treat you well. If you are not confident, and do not take care of yourself, you often will attract losers and abusers.

Chapter 6:

Secret Key #5

Give and Take on the Lead

This key is one of the most secret keys there are, because most people don't realize that the man doesn't always wear the pants in a relationship. You both have to make the big decisions together, and take turns on the smaller ones. You cannot let one single person take control of the relationship. If you work together, you unlock a bond that allows him to see you as an equal and not as below him.

If you make all of the decisions in the relationship, you allow him to be passive, but if he makes all the decisions, you become passive. Neither one of you should become passive, because this is a one way ticket to a controlling relationship. While it does not always end up that way, fifty six percent of relationships where one person is in charge of most or all of the decisions turn into be abusive relationships.

The solution to avoid this problem is to take turns making decisions. Even the smaller decisions like where to go when you go out to eat, or what to watch on television. On the bigger decisions, make them together. Especially on whether or not to buy a house or start a family, or any big purchase.

Also, take care of finances together, or split them up equally. You cannot give one person complete control of the finances, and expect to not have some control issues. Money is the biggest player in a controlling relationship. If one person has all the control of the money, they can tell the other partner what they can and cannot do, and once you get a taste of that power, it escalates from there.

The best way to avoid this is to get a joint account if you are married that has both of your names on it, so you both can access the funds, or have separate accounts with only your name on it, so the other partner can't access the funds. If you do this though, you have to decide how to split the bills. Otherwise, there will be issues with bills not getting paid, and utilities being shut off. This is if you live together. If not, you don't have to worry about it.

If you don't want to take turns on even the little decisions, then work together to decide everything. From where you want to eat, to where you want to live. Working together will create a strong bond between you two as well. You will grow closer together as you achieve things together. Think about it. If you make great strides in your life with the one you love, who are you going to celebrate with? That's right, them. So it only makes sense that if you make all your decisions together, you will grow closer due to the fact that you celebrate every achievement as one. You have to want to work together though, otherwise, you will argue more than you work together.

Why is this Key Important?

You want to unlock his heart in a way that makes him see you as an equal rather than a lesser, as society tries to make everyone think. If he sees you as his equal, he will learn to depend on you, rather than walk all over you. There will be less debates on who should make what decisions, and who is always right, because you will both be able to compromise and work together to achieve a blissful relationship.

Breakthrough With Women

Women are a puzzle for men to figure out. Just as women have to figure out men. Each person is a different puzzle and when you find the piece that fits, you have a long lasting relationship. Figuring out the secret to women or the woman you are currently in a relationship with—is easier than ever.

You have a guide that will help you think about the women you are typically interested in dating, currently dating or even married to. Just because you succeed in marrying a woman does not mean the work is over. Marriage is work. Any relationship takes work and involvement.

As a secret key, you cannot expect it to work with every woman you meet. Some women are simply unwilling to open their hearts. You will be given the tools to recognize when a woman is close-hearted, so you know that she is the wrong person for you.

The one thing you cannot forget as you read through this guide—is that you have to decide how much work you are willing to put into the relationship you wish to have. If you are reading this guide hoping you can unlock a woman's heart and then wish to become complacent, your relationship is doomed from the beginning.

Some women also take more work than others. They can have complicated lives or enjoy a little "too much" drama in how they act; therefore, you have to decide what you want in a relationship to gain a serious long term commitment.

You probably didn't think that you are part of the secret key. Yet, you are. Chemistry will only take you so far. A long term relationship, where the woman gives you her full heart begins with you.

So why do you need these "secret keys?" You need them because you want to unlock a woman's heart to its full potential. You want your relationship to go beyond the normal level because you want to be among the 10% who are blissfully happy. Only men who discover the secret of how a woman thinks, what she wants, and her ultimate desire to open her heart to the right man, will be among the elite happy couples in the world.

Discover the path to finally gain access to the "one's" heart that you wish to spend the rest of your life with, through the good and the bad.

CHAPTER 1

WHAT DO YOU WANT?

Do you walk into an electronics store or a car dealership without knowing what you want? No, if you are like most men, you buy magazines that tell you all the technical specs about the latest technology and cars. You also go online to forums and tech websites to do research.

Why would you try to pick up women or try dating sites without knowing what you want? You do not want to do that. If you are like most men, then you have dated, enjoyed one-night stands, and explored the pool of women.

Now, you are reading this book because you are looking for something more. Perhaps, you haven't dated more than a few women and wonder what you are doing wrong?

The men who are successful in relationships, who find those long term marriages—they are the ones who know what they want.

I'll give you an example of a marriage that lasted 42 years. It would have lasted longer if illness did not exist. This couple met when the wife moved into a new apartment complex with two other female friends. The young man, at the time, came up to see if there was anyone he wanted to date or would want to go on dates with him.

He would call up the night he wanted to date and see if someone was willing. He even spent eight months in another state. But, this man realized he had met the one person for him in that apartment.

He came back from living in a different place with one thing in mind—to ensure this woman would date him. He tried his nonchalant style, calling up the day of to ask for a date. She would always refuse because she also had other plans already in the works.

Finally, this man asked, "what do I have to do to get you to go out with me?"

The answer was simple, "call in advance."

The couple dated a few times before Christmas, every week during January and were engaged the day before Valentines.

Life doesn't always happen this way, but you can be

sure that the man knew what he wanted. He dated several women, going out when they were available, and enjoying coffee, a meal, or a movie. But, no one caught his attention as much as the woman he married. It took distance to realize that no other woman compared.

If you have not dated very many people, then you need to get out there. You need to start dating more. How else are you supposed to figure out what you want?

I'll give you another example. This couple was together for 17 years and married for 13, almost 14 years. The marriage ended with a divorce and two suffering children. The man dated only two people, marrying the second. The woman had dated more men, but also enjoyed being the center of attention, the person that knows it all, and the person who lies because she doesn't recognize the truth. When the husband asked her father for her hand, the father said, "she is just like her mother, are you sure you know what you are doing?" Her mother constantly spends every dime that is earned, is all about herself, and often depressed and unhappy. Of course, the husband thought he could live with it all, only to find that the woman he was marrying could easily ask for a divorce and immediately move in with another man.

The lesson in this second example is—you can know what you want and what you are capable of living with, but you also have to make allowances for the other person.

A person who cannot love themselves will never be able to love another with their whole heart.

Are you willing to accept being second or loved with less than a whole heart? Are you willing to date or marry someone when, you know, eventually, it will come to an end, it's just a matter of how long it takes?

These are the questions you need to ask yourself as

you begin to learn the secrets to enter a woman's heart completely. Only when you know yourself and what you are willing to accept, can you truly find your way into the right woman's heart.

CHAPTER 2

SECRET KEY #1

Open, Honest, Consistent Communication

Pick up a woman's magazine that has a quiz. I bet that quiz has a section on communication. It probably tests the woman on how communicative her partner is and offers advice on how to elicit more communication. There are millions of these quizzes and articles in magazines, online, and they are all designed for woman by woman. Yet, you can learn something from this concept. Why do you think communication is such a hot topic? It is because women are fundamentally different from men.

Women can be extremely intuitive, even read body language, but women still consider the way men think a mystery. Women cannot believe a man is only thinking about sex. There has to be something more in your brains, right? You are capable of multitasking at your job, of dating multiple women, and holding deep conversations on politics, religion, engineering or something equally complicated—so you must have more on your mind than sex.

You also have feelings. These feelings can be hurt. You can also be excited and feel love. Women are unable to understand why you are unable to talk about these deeper feelings, and demand that you do.

A group of women get together and they catch up. What has happened in your life, what are you doing now, what happened last week. The conversation invariably turns to emotions, but it is not the whole discussion.

Women seek other women for emotional support and understanding because they feel they lack it from the men in their life. Women also work on hormones more so than men.

It's a fact and not something you should fear discussing. A woman can be happy one moment and the wrong words can flip a switch. The grudge can be held for days with the wrong words. A man usually forgets about the issue in a few hours or days, unless the same thing keeps happening.

So, on one hand, women have a need to know your emotions because they cannot understand them unless you tell them. On the other, there are emotional mind fields that you have to navigate as you communicate.

It has been the experience of most women that men do not want to communicate about their feelings. They find it a waste of time. Yet, it is the one thing that will help your woman feel confident in the relationship. It is the way for you to work your way into their heart.

The key is for this communication to be open, honest and consistent.

Defining Open

What does open communication mean? In business, it is a setting where employees are encouraged to share their thoughts and concerns, without the fear of retaliation (reference.com). In a relationship, it is the same thing, only the thoughts and concerns to be shared are about personal situations.

Communication includes issues about one's job, the treatment of the person by their boss, monetary concerns, kids, religion, love, and all other feelings people have.

For example, a family of four sat around a dinner table to discuss whether a move to a new state would be the best option for their family. The discussion included the changes that would occur, the employment options for the parents, and why the move would offer monetary stability versus the current place they lived. Each person was given a chance to discuss their thoughts, fears, concerns, and acceptance of the move.

Another family of four also moved. In this family, the parents sat their children down, said they were moving, and stated where. No communication from the children was allowed as to how they felt or why a move had to occur.

Do you think the children in the first family were more prepared and less unsettled than the second family? Of course, they were. They weighed in with their opinion, fears, concerns, and desires. The second family's children had to keep what they thought to themselves.

Now, consider this example, as a communication between two people: You have two people in a relationship, where one person is always stating what is going to happen, without giving reasons or why it is the best? How unsettled will the partner be? How angry do you think they will become at not having a choice?

Open communication is required to help your woman understand how you think, the reasons behind your actions, and to feel secure in the relationship. If you do not share your thoughts and feelings, how are they to know what you are really thinking? How are they to feel secure that you truly care about them, if they are not kept in the loop or considered part of the equation.

The game telephone provides a good example of this concept. One person starts a statement and by the end of ten or twenty people the statement has changed drastically. By the time your body signals based on your emotions are translated by a woman, they are changed because she is going to interpret them based on how she thinks, just like you try to interpret her behavior based on how you think.

Without communication, you are unable to figure out what each of you is thinking.

Honest Communication

Does this outfit make me look fat? Yes. Ouch. But, it is also how you deliver the answer. You need to be honest because there is one thing a woman does not want—she doesn't want to wear something that does not look good and she will feel embarrassed about later on. Also, here is the kicker—if you lie about how she looks in an outfit—what else could you be lying about?

It is far better to tell the truth when asked for it, then to lie. Furthermore, it is 100% better to speak the truth in any situation. If there is a behavior that bothers you, speak up. One woman told her husband this, "If I start acting like my mother, tell me." She was fearful that she would start displaying certain negative behavior that her mother had and she didn't want to. She was always hurt when being told "you are acting like your mother," but it also helped her realize that a correction to her behavior was required.

A woman who loves herself and gives of herself, completely, to the man she loves is capable of accepting the truth. The anger and stewing for a few hours is better than ignoring the problem or lying to avoid conflict.

Now will all women agree, no. Some women are unable to take the hurt that honest communication provides, but ask yourself, do you want a woman who can give her whole heart because she values your honesty or the woman who keeps a grudge and eventually causes too much pain?

You want the woman who can give her whole heart, so be honest in your communication and explain why you will always tell the truth, even if it is not what the person wants to hear. You'll be valued for this behavior because you are noticing and trying, as well as remaining truthful.

Consistency

More times than I have fingers I have seen relationships start where each person is honest, and communicative. However, after a year or two, the communication stops being consistent. It is like each man and woman believe they have figured the person out and know what they are thinking, so it is less necessary to be communicative.

Wrong.

You cannot become complacent just because it seems like the woman is not demanding communication as often as she was. There are only a few reasons she feels communication is no longer as necessary:

- She thinks she knows you well enough that she can read your moods.

- She is no longer interested.

- She is angry when you don't truly communicate.

If it is the first, then you need to show her that talking each night before you go to sleep is important to you. You need to give of yourself for her to continue giving of herself.

If she is no longer interested, you need to know, so you can move on to find the right person. Sometimes a woman has just as much difficulty breaking off a relationship. She doesn't want to cause hurt when she is unwilling to give her whole heart.

The last reason is fairly easy to discern. If you have not provided any worthwhile communication, then she will turn away, say "fine, whatever," or something along those words and stop trying to communicate with you.

For communication to unlock your woman's heart, you need to:

- Learn to read body language
- Read the subtle nuances in her tone
- And give of yourself before you ask her to give of herself

If you are embarrassed about your thoughts because they are just about "sex" in that moment—don't be. Tell her. But more than anything, have a time of day when the two of you talk about what happened at work, the challenges or the good things, and plans that you have or things that you want to do.

The conversation does not have to be deep and always about emotions each night. Rather, you are supposed to come together, be honest, be consistent, and just share. You are not to judge, just to listen, with attentiveness. If you only hear the words, then you cannot repeat them.

Here is something else that is usually a complaint from a guy, "all she has ever said are complaints. We never talk about anything other than how much she hates this or that."

Did you ever think that perhaps she is not happy with something that could be changed? Perhaps she needs a new perspective? Maybe, feelings of unhappiness in other areas of her life are making her complain about something else? The biggest one—did you ever think that she only communicates when there is something negative?

Try it, if you are already in a relationship. Track your communication for a week. Did your woman want to talk when she was happy or did she only want to talk when something was bothering her? Did you try to get her to talk about her day or the happy stuff, or did you think "yay, I don't have to try communicating today?"

Your effort to get her to talk when she is happy, will be rewarded. She will know that she can talk about anything, but more that you care to listen about everything. She will learn to talk about the good and the bad, so you don't hear only the unhappy things.

Thus, the ultimate secret is your effort in getting her to communicate about all things, just as much as she is asking you to communicate about anything at all.

One man said, "I didn't think you wanted to listen. I figured it would bore you."

His statement was definitely an insight into why he lacked communication. It was also the key his partner needed to understand that she needed to put more effort into listening.

Most try to say that communication is a two-way street, but is it really? If you drive on a two-way street, you have to keep to your own lane to avoid an accident. I suppose you could "meet in the middle," and block traffic. I'd rather think of communication as a one-way street. One of you has to be illegally driving to meet in the middle, but sometimes that is what it takes for a heart to open. If you are not willing to put in the effort to circumvent any blocks in the way, such as illegally driving down a one-way street, then how can you open up her heart?

She will see the motivation and honesty in your effort to communicate on all subjects that are important to you and her, not just what may be important to her. This will open her heart a little further, and allow her to trust in your feelings for her.

CHAPTER 3

SECRET KEY #2

Equality and Respect

This is a chapter that should be common sense, but more often than not, it is not. Countries were founded on inequality and there are many still struggling with inequality issues to the point that women are killed if they step out of line. Given how sensitive a topic this is—it should not surprise you that all women want to be treated equally and with respect.

Yes, there are people with more intellect than others, but talking down to them or disrespecting them is not the proper way to communicate. What if you were faced with a woman who had an IQ of 185 and she consistently talked down to you even about simple topics? A man's pride gets pricked pretty easy. It is annoying when a woman is or acts smarter than you. So, why wouldn't it be annoying and insensitive if you are always acting smarter than the woman you are with.

Here is an example: A young man not very well versed in subtle body language and common sense would talk about simple things, a topic that he had in common with a young woman. But, he would often use an arrogant tone with an "I know more than you" attitude. He would tell this young woman things she already knew, like she didn't know the first thing about it.

The relationship didn't last. Nor will any relationship in this situation, when the woman is capable of knowing herself, her own intellect, and a proper way of having a conversation.

It doesn't have to always be about conversation, either. It is just an easy example that helps shore up the previous chapter.

When you communicate in a relationship, the woman wants to be seen as your equal, to have an equal opinion. She doesn't want her words discounted because you know better.

She wants her words to resonate, for you to think about them, and help explain why something else would be better or why her opinion is valued, but not the right approach.

For example, let's say you are married and you have a child. Your child starts to refuse to eat. You might have a different viewpoint than your wife. Your wife might allow the child to go to bed without food until the child finally figures out that starving is not the answer. You might not want your child to go to bed hungry, so you will allow your child to choose a healthy snack such as apples and cheese.

Your wife feels that you are giving in to your child and their refusal to eat healthy things. You might feel that letting your child go hungry, can have unhealthy consequences. Who is right or wrong? That is not the answer. The question is who is going to see results quicker? If the father will get the child to eat healthy foods, then the child will remain healthy. If the child continues to not eat enough, even with healthy snacks then this can hinder the path to a solution. Whereas, starving often gets a child to eat, even a little of something they don't like or a willingness to try it cooked a different way in order to never go to bed hungry again.

The debate won't be answered here because the point is not to solve the question, but to realize that if you refuse to listen to your partner's opinion, harm could be done in more ways than one. You could end up hurting your child and on the other hand, you are putting your wife in a position of disrespect in front of the child.

Dismissing what your partner, whether you are dating, going to the next step, or married, is not going to get her to open her heart to you. Are you always right 100% of the time in all areas? Of course not, and neither is your partner.

The key is for you two to be able to see each other as equals. You look at each other, know your strengths and weaknesses, and compromise when necessary, but never with a disrespectful attitude.

It is okay to point out certain mistakes, but make sure you do it with respect. Value the person and they will open their heart to you. They will also value you more, for showing that you value them.

If you have not yet noticed this is leading to "trust." For a woman to give their entire heart to you—they need to trust you, trust that you understand them, respect them, and value what they have to say or to give in the relationship.

Communication is not the only way to make this known. Body language is also very important in a woman being seen as an equal. If you ignore something they say or do, it is an act of disrespect, of seeing them as less.

For you it may be complacency. You might be used to the person always cooking your dinner, so you forget to say thank you or take notice of their hard work. The husband or boyfriend who is successful never lets anything go unnoticed.

Car Doors and Other Doors

"She has her own hands; she can open the door."

Have you ever thought this? Perhaps you know someone who has? Maybe, the women you have dated told you it is unnecessary to open doors for her?

Yes, a woman likes to do for herself, but that doesn't mean you should never open a door for her. Choose your moments. Make it a surprise. Even a woman who is capable and willing to open her own doors, appreciates when a gentleman will do it for her. It is based on when you open the door.

For instance, let's say your girlfriend has her arms full of things and there is no hand to open the door. You would immediately open it for her, right? Of course.

The next time you need to open the door is when you are taking her out for a special dinner.

"Let me get the door." This statement tells her that you appreciate that she is coming with you and that she has dressed lovely for the evening. It is a "special" occasion that supersedes the usual rule that she will open her own doors.

If you are running late and it is easier for your partner to open her door, then wait and she doesn't mind opening her own door—it is okay to let her. If she is the type that always needs the door open as a sign of chivalry, then you still, have to open it.

It is not about the door. It is about the effort and respect such an action provides. Again, you let the woman make a choice based on her preferences or you simply ask what she prefers. You choose your moments to be sweet or you always show respect because that is what your heart tells you to do.

There are men who will tell a woman, "I was raised to open

doors as a sign of respect. Not complying with this, goes against the respect I have for you."

The key again is to communicate what you know to be right, so that your partner also understands your point of view.

You should back down to show your respect, but also in the same light tell her that you are respecting her more by following through with certain instincts.

Remember these suggestions are examples. You have your upbringing and your partner will have hers. As long as you show mutual respect for each other, and equality of the minds, then you will have a woman who is willing to show you her heart.

CHAPTER 4

SECRET KEY #3

Acceptance for Who They Are

What is the one thing many women have tried to do when they started dating you? They tried to change you. The wrong woman always tries to change her partner. They want you to fit into an ideal they have for a man. There are plenty of reasons for this.

- She is afraid of never finding someone who will accept her

- She feels you are broken and in need of fixing

The two bullet points are the two main reasons she may try to change you. A smart woman will eventually realize that she cannot change the man she is dating. She has to accept him for who he is, his faults and strengths, or find someone else.

You may wish to change the woman you are dating too. Perhaps she doesn't care enough about her appearance? Maybe, she shops and spends too much money? It may be something simple that you do not like, but cannot seem to ignore.

You have an option. You can stop dating a person because she has habits or traits you cannot ignore or you can accept them. It is your choice, but you need to make it.

Don't stay with someone because of your own fear. Yes, men do have fears. There are men out there who fear that they will have to settle for one woman because the one they want is unattainable. Did you ever think that you are not settling, but finding the person who is right for you? Do not settle if things do not feel right and in the same vain do not choose a woman who you cannot accept for her faults and strengths.

If you already have problems or fights due to basic personality clashes, then you are not going to get the woman to stay with you and give her full heart.

The secret is to truly accept, no matter what or to realize that you cannot. If you can accept all of her faults, then you will open her heart a little more, and eventually her whole heart will be yours.

The one thing you cannot do is change your mind and expect her to open her heart. She has to know that there is consistency within your own heart. You either accept her for who she is or you don't. If you do not really accept her faults, then you will always have doubts in your mind. You will always question or find yourself focusing on the things you cannot accept.

People can only change themselves if they see a problem. They are not going to change because you want the change to happen. For a time, they may try to be better, but after a while, their inherent traits will win out. There is no way around the traits winning, unless the person they are a part of is willing to change.

Yes, you received an example earlier that stated the wife wanted to know when she was acting like her mother. The key here is that she wanted to know. She asked for the truth. She was already in the frame of mind that she may need to change her behavior if she became like her mother.

If you try to point out things to a woman who has not asked or does not think there is something wrong within herself, then you are not going to succeed. She will close her heart and doubt that you can love her fully when you cannot accept all of who she is.

There is also a difference in accepting who a woman is and being her support for the changes that she wishes to make.

What if the woman you are dating had a bad family experience as a child? What if she lacks confidence? Can you deal with her frame of mind and self-doubt? What if you could be her support to help her build her self-confidence without actually pointing out that she needs the help?

It is possible. If you are open and willing to accept the woman for who she is and the potential of who she desires to be, then you are going to find her whole heart is in your hands.

By now you should see a theme in the secrets to a woman's heart: trust and support.

Any woman you date needs to feel they can trust you and that you will be supportive. Without trust and support, she is going to feel like you are only partially in the relationship and she is going to hold back.

It does not matter how many relationships you have had that reach the next level from dating casually to steadily. It does not matter if you have married before and your marriage has failed or is struggling. If you can provide trust and support for the woman you value in your life, you will finally succeed in opening her complete heart to you.

The Pedestal

One man succeeded and another did not. There was a time when one woman was dating two men. She would go out on Fridays with one guy and Saturdays with the other. Both men knew she was dating someone else, but they had never met. One man asked for her hand and was given a "yes." The other took her to a wrestling match the day she received the marriage proposal. The next date he found out she was going to marry the other guy and asked, "are you sure. I love you, you are everything to me, I've put you on a pedestal and don't know how I can live without you being my wife."

The woman's answer: "Your first mistake was putting me on a pedestal."

No one wants to be on a pedestal.

Already it was mentioned that you need to accept the woman for who she is. A part of this discussion is about that very concept. You do need to accept a woman's faults.

More importantly, you cannot raise a woman too higher than she truly is. You cannot have a "celebrity" image of the woman you wish to date.

What if every woman went around trying to find her perfect guy from the romance novels she reads or the songs that have been sung?

You know she won't find this guy because you know men have faults and are not romantic heroes like in the books and movies.

You cannot put a woman on a pedestal and expect a life of happiness to follow.

The minute you put a woman on a pedestal is the minute your relationship is wrong.

You have to be supportive and help her learn to trust you, but you cannot make her a "goddess," in your mind.

Do not keep the rose colored glasses on and reference what you truly want.

What do you wish to see in a woman you can spend your life with? Are you the type of man who needs space, but will never stray? Can you look at attractive women, but know that the one beside you, is the most attractive because of the entire package? If so, then you don't need a pedestal for her. You just need to marry her if you haven't already.

CHAPTER 5

SECRET KEY #4

The Pedestal

One man succeeded and another did not. There was a time when one woman was dating two men. She would go out on Fridays with one guy and Saturdays with the other. Both men knew she was dating someone else, but they had never met. One man asked for her hand and was given a "yes." The other took her to a wrestling match the day she received the marriage proposal. The next date he found out she was going to marry the other guy and asked, "are you sure. I love you, you are everything to me, I've put you on a pedestal and don't know how I can live without you being my wife."

The woman's answer: "Your first mistake was putting me on a pedestal."

No one wants to be on a pedestal.

Already it was mentioned that you need to accept the woman for who she is. A part of this discussion is about that very concept. You do need to accept a woman's faults.

More importantly, you cannot raise a woman too higher than she truly is. You cannot have a "celebrity" image of the woman you wish to date.

What if every woman went around trying to find her perfect guy from the romance novels she reads or the songs that have been sung?

You know she won't find this guy because you know men have faults and are not romantic heroes like in the books and movies.

You cannot put a woman on a pedestal and expect a life of happiness to follow.

The minute you put a woman on a pedestal is the

minute your relationship is wrong.

You have to be supportive and help her learn to trust you, but you cannot make her a "goddess," in your mind.

Do not keep the rose colored glasses on and reference what you truly want.

What do you wish to see in a woman you can spend your life with? Are you the type of man who needs space, but will never stray? Can you look at attractive women, but know that the one beside you, is the most attractive because of the entire package? If so, then you don't need a pedestal for her. You just need to marry her if you haven't already.

CHAPTER 6

SECRET KEY #5

Make Her Smile

The key to most women's hearts is to make her smile and laugh. The right woman will accept your personality, whether it is sarcastic humor or witty humor. It is also the effort you provide in making her smile or laugh. For example, a coworker recently knew his female coworker was having a bad day. They are friends and nothing more, as there is a significant difference in age. Yet, the man, going through his own trials, still worked for a good hour to make her laugh and smile rather than to continue crying as she was doing.

This is a man who understands that humor, even in making silly faces, giving out zinger, witty remarks, is the key to making a woman fall a little in love, even if it is only friendship.

You don't have to be the wittiest. You may have a stupid joke that makes one groan more than laugh or smile. However, the effort in trying to make the woman smile, to make her laugh, will instantly make her heart melt.

Gifts are Important

Surprise gifts are important to a woman. They consider these gifts as supportive or endearing because you are paying attention to her. There are times when life gets routine, mundane, and even filled with complacency on both of your sides. The trick is to come home with a surprise.

Flowers are nice for some women. For others, they are an instant allergy issue. Some men feel that flowers are going to die, so why spend the money, when something else can be provided, such as a vacation from saving money on the little things.

The key is to know what your woman believes and what you can do that will matter to her heart. Sometimes it can be the silliest thing or the simplest. What if you both love tattoos? Did you ever think about getting a tattoo of a symbol or date that matters to both of you?

Perhaps, it is as simple as coming home with a card. Maybe when she goes on a business trip you hide a card in her bag moments before you say goodbye at the airport.

Gifts do not have to be expensive, they do not have to

be jewelry, but they do need to be thought of and given. Yes, some women prefer expensive gifts, even demand them, and if you have a wife or partner like this, then you need to comply sometimes. It goes back to accepting and knowing the woman you have in your life. However, it doesn't mean that small things like cards and spontaneous gifts that are not expensive won't move her heart.

It is all about what you know about her desires, what she is used to, and what will make her smile and love you because of the effort you have shown. You can also show a woman used to expensive gifts that it is not the money, but the honesty behind the gift that matters the most.

CHAPTER 7

Special Bonus Tips

Not all women will fit your personality. There are some women who should not be in relationships or marry, unless they can find a partner who is just like them in the key ways. There are even some women who will never open their heart and find true happiness because they cannot find it in themselves. These bonus tips will help you look at relationships and women, so you might succeed, when you have faced certain issues such as being in a bad relationship, failing to be supportive in small ways, or even noticing her each and every day.

Things to Look Out For

- Does your current partner feel love is shown through how much you buy her?

- Does she flirt with other men to see if you are getting angry or noticing what she is doing?

- Does she seem to pick a fight or get angry for no reason you can see?

- Has she started to withdraw from you?

- Is she starting to ignore you, your phone calls, or breaking dates?

These are a few signs that you need to look out for in understanding that she is not the woman for you. Some of these can also be a sign that she may have a psychological issue that she cannot get passed and will eventually affect the relationship.

For instance, have you ever date a woman who lies, who tries to separate you from friends and family, needs "things" to feel you love her, and is always thinking about herself? This can be the sign of a narcissist. A narcissist is someone who views themselves as the most important, cannot handle when someone else is more important, is often arrogant, and knows everything. This same person also blames everyone around them for being at fault and for doing things they are actually doing.

Toxic relationships like this need to be avoided, even if you feel you can live with this person's faults. Drama is another word that has been applied to women who seem to cause conflict, always pick a fight, and have a healthy sexual appetite that never seems satisfied with just one person.

Only you can truly say what type of relationship you are looking for, but there are definitely signs that you need to watch out for with regards to women and drama they can create.

- A woman can call you several times a day or demand that you call them often.

- They may ask where you were and not trust your answer.

- They may text or try to start up a conversation that is too deep on the first meeting.

- They may complain and find nothing happy.

These are just a few other signs that a woman may not be right for you or perhaps anyone. Someone who is obsessive without actually dating you can have psychological issues that require a professional. It may not be nice to say of one's own sex, but it is also the truth. Some women need to recognize their failings and accept those in order to find a healthy relationship, otherwise they are "crazy" in their actions towards men, bordering on obsessive.

Signs of a Wrong Relationship

Relationships do not have to be filled with "crazy" or drama to be wrong for you. There are definite signs that a woman is not right for you, when she is unwilling to give her heart to you. It is not a matter of you trying harder to be supportive, and not complacent in the relationship.

Here is an example of a woman. See if you can see why she might be wrong for a relationship with you.

- She prefers her own company to others.

- She has social anxiety.

- She needs a routine and does not like that routine to be interrupted.

- She is hyper-organized, hating when someone fills up a space she just cleaned.

- She cannot trust easily.

- She is unwilling to be hurt and face the loss of a husband, preferring to die before any of her family, so she doesn't have to face that horrible situation.

- She also has a dislike of touch, something no one can pinpoint a cause for, but one that holds her from a deep physical relationship.

Obviously, this is an extreme example, but take note of it. Sometimes the signs are subtle and other times there is a big sign saying "this is not right." A woman who does not allow physical contact after three dates either has issues with physical contact or does not see you as a sexual partner. A relationship that is not right for you will have fights, ups and downs, and disagreements on the main issues. You won't be able to agree on politics, religion, children, and life in general.

Additional Effort Options

A couple was having trouble in their marriage. The wife was unhappy. The man knew it, but couldn't figure out what to do. He decided he would ask her each morning, "what can I do to make your day better?" At first, his wife thought he was being insensitive and joking. After he kept asking she realized that he meant it and started answering, as well as asking how she could make his day better.

Such a simple phrase and the care behind it saved the marriage. You can do something like this in your relationship. It doesn't have to be a big deal. It can be something as simple as asking how your partner's day was or how you can make it better.

It can also be something that will make her smile. The married couple of 42 years is another great example. One child was grown, married, and nearing having children. The second child left home to live 3,000 miles away. Living as just the two of them, the wife was missing her children. To make her day better, the husband took one of the stuffed animals his daughter left when she moved away, and started creating funny scenes.

One day the orangutan stuffed animal was holding a fake cigarette and reading in their bed. The next day it was playing chess with one of the wife's stuffed bears of similar size. For over a week, the husband would wake up, create a scene, leave for work, and his wife would come home to it. She would smile. Now she has pictures of these scenes to help her memory, since the husband passed away from early onset dementia.

These little efforts changed the wife's outlook for the day, the ache in her heart from missing her daughter, and now is a comfort to her with him gone.

What can you think to do that would have such a lasting impact because it is guaranteed to open the woman's heart for life.

Flowers are acceptable, of course, and even desired by most women. But, if you have the imagination, find something that can truly make her smile, laugh, or even cry with happiness. It matters.

Helping Your Partner become a Better Her

The couple who spent 42 years together respected each other, loved each other, and were best friends as well as husband and wife. One of the biggest impacts the husband had on his wife, was mutual respect, equality, and the power to give her what made her a better version of herself. This is not about changing the person, but giving her the tools to go after what she desires.

The wife was told by her mother on more than one occasion that she was stupid, worthless and that her mother wished she had never been born. Her only choice of work was to go to a trade school. Given the year she graduated, her only real choice was to become a hairdresser. It was not something she hated, but her husband also gave her the choice of being able to do more and spend more time with her children as they grew.

In fact, she started working with her husband on construction sites building houses as a family. It gave her more freedom to spend with her children, as well as spend every day with her husband. When she would ask can "I do this or do that," such as take ballet, he told her "you never have to ask. You can do what you want to do."

He gave her the power to try different things and be who she was, without judgement. It helped that they had the money for her to try new things, but all the same he told her they were equal that the money they made was hers to spend as she wished.

Now, she was also brought up in a poor family, so spending money was a difficult decision. She never spent money that was earmarked for bills, groceries, and necessary monthly expenses. She was responsible in the spending, but also given the chance to explore and do.

It made her heart open more for this husband. You may find that you are drawn to such a woman yourself. You also need to realize that while she is becoming a better version of herself because of you, she can also make you a better version of yourself. It is not about changing who you are inherently, but about taking what you are, loving who you are, and helping you be the best you can be even in the face of adversity.

The person who can allow this and accept such help in return is the person that can form a long term, lasting relationship with the right woman. It is also the person who will have the whole heart of the woman he loves.

Withholding Due to Fear

A lack of support and trust in a relationship can lead to the woman you are dating or married to, fearing to give her whole heart to you. There are subtle signs you need to look for if the woman fears giving her heart.

- She will withhold herself too.

- She will often go on trips without you for business or to visit family, and not call.

- She will test to see if she can live without you.

- She will test you in communication to be more open in conversation.

- She will become angry or distant if you answer wrong or continue to withhold.

- More fights will occur.

- She will start to ask where you see the relationship going.

These are fear tests that she is giving you. She is hoping that you will realize her fear and start to open up, start to pay attention, and show her through action not words, how much she means to you.

If she is not the right woman, then don't let her live in fear. If she is the woman you wish to gain her whole heart, recognize the fear, address it, and start changing how you communicate, offer her your trust, and support.

What do you do if a woman says she is moving out? Do you let her or do you ask her what is going on?

If you have established open communication, where she feels she can trust you, but is not receiving proper support or respect, she will tell you her fear. If you have done nothing to gain her trust, respect, support, or communication she will be evasive and tell you "it's just not working or it's me not you."

For the right woman, you will strive to correct

yourself to make her more comfortable and recognize your fault and the fear of the relationship she is feeling. If you cannot give her that, then you need to allow the relationship to end, learn from it, and start looking for the woman who is right for you.

Are you Clinging

There are certain turn offs for a woman.

- She does not want to be your mother.
- She does not want to constantly clean up after you.
- She does not want to cook you every meal you eat.
- She wants you to make an effort.
- She does not want you to call 10 times a day.
- She wants you to respect what she says and remember what she says.

- If she tells you no, then it is no. Not maybe, not flirting, not suggestive.

- If she asks for your opinion or a decision on what you want to do—give her one.

- A woman wants a decisive man, who knows himself, and is not afraid to laugh at himself.

Above all she does not want a man who clings. She does not want someone who is obtuse to her feelings or the subtle information she is giving him. She wants someone who is willing to pay attention, to be supportive, who will try to gain her trust, and love her so she can open her heart to him.

The secret to breakthrough with women are simple — create a situation where you are supportive and gain her trust. To be the one, you have to give of yourself before you ask her to give you all of herself.

Each woman is different in personality, tastes, and needs, but they are also fundamentally the same in needing to be important, respected, equal in mind and body, and loved unconditionally.

Only when you can be yourself, honest, supportive,

and respect her fully can you be "the one" for her.

You also have to realize that sometimes a woman is unwilling to open her heart. Sometimes she may not see you as the one or no matter what you do to try opening her heart, she simply cannot.

If you can recognize that she is never going to open her heart to you, then you can move on to a woman who is willing.

Sometimes you definitely get lucky and met the "one" for you and marry three months later. Sometimes it takes years. You have to be open. You have to be willing. You cannot be complacent. You also have to know what you are looking for to recognize her when she comes along.

If you don't know your own mind, then you won't be able to see the woman who is right for you. She could be next to you, waiting for you to see her and waiting to open her heart to you. She may be the next woman you meet through an online dating service.

Only when you have the secret key to making sure you are supportive and giving her a reason to trust you—will you succeed.

www.ingramcontent.com/pod-product-compliance
Lightning Source LLC
LaVergne TN
LVHW010317070526
838199LV00065B/5593